THE SEARCH
FOR TROLLHAVEN

THE SEARCH FOR TROLLHAVEN

Odd Bjerke and Meredith Motson

Illustrated by Marvin Wood

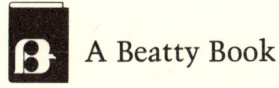
A Beatty Book

ISBN 0-916238-06-7
Library of Congress Catalog Card Number: 77-77794
R. O. Beatty & Associates, P.O. Box 763, Boise, Idaho 83702
Copyright © 1977 by Odd Bjerke and Meredith Motson
Illustrations © 1977 by R. O. Beatty & Associates, Inc.
All rights reserved
Printed in the United States of America

If Ever . . .	1
The Sixteenth of May	7
Farvel	16
Islands on the Ice	27
God Jul	38
The Leader in the Lead	49
Okpiks and Kiwitaks	58
Bowheads and Iceboats	66
Nesa's Nose	76
The Lore of the Southlands	85
The Eagle's Way	96
Ee-da-how	109
Velkommen	117
Touched by a Tail	129
Autumn Turns	138
The Call of the Mountain	147
The Magic Language	156
And So . . .	167
Guide to Norwegian Pronunciation	170

If Ever . . .

If ever you happen to travel to Norway, you will hear of a place where three rivers meet. Vågå, Lesja and Lom they are called, and where they join is a lake called Sperillen.

The lake is easy enough to find if you take the road sixty kilometers from Oslo. Then, making your way through the birch and pine forests, you will see a mountain known as Troll Tinderne. Here you should definitely stop awhile, for this mountain, as you may have already guessed, is the meeting place of the trolls and where our tale begins.

Spring in troll country! High on Troll Tinderne the snow had almost disappeared, and down at the lake only a few patches of white remained. Up through them poked bluebells and lilies of the valley, and red and white heather waved from the mountain.

Suddenly the mountain's reflection rippled on the lake. Something whispered in the birch trees along the shore, and drops began to fall, slipping from one leaf to the next, using the leaves as a stairway to the ground below. From deep in the woods came the tap of the woodpecker, and over the lake rang the cry of the loon.

The bushes rustled. The animals twitched. At the doors of their hollows they sniffed the wind. There was more in the air than the gentle rain. Yes, they were sure! And off they ran to spread the news: it was May sixteenth!

You see, the next day, the seventeenth of May, is Norwegian Independence Day, when all over Norway the people celebrate. But the eve of Independence Day is even more important. At dusk the animals meet at Lake Sperillen, and at midnight on the mountain is the Council of the Trolls.

But wait! Here we're already talking of trolls, when you may not know the first thing about them—like why they wait until midnight to hold their most important meeting of the year. You see, trolls have a very serious problem. If they stand in bright sunlight very long, they suddenly explode and turn to stone!

Lady trolls have a special problem of their own. Their knees don't bend quite as far as the men's, so when they climb mountains they're always stubbing their toes. This causes terrible ingrown toenails. Ingrown toenails ache, and what is worse, the only remedy is birch bark sap mixed to a froth with reindeer milk. You can imagine the bother it is having to go way up to Lapland to milk reindeer, but that's another thing you have to put up with if you are a troll.

Perhaps you already know that trolls live in the Scandinavian countries of Norway, Sweden and Denmark. Finland is not really Scandinavian, but a few small forest trolls have been spotted there, mostly around the edges of Lake Ladoga.

The forest trolls are the largest. Generally they can be found in the provinces of Valdres, Gudbrandsdalen and Gaustad, where they are known to grow over sixty feet tall. Like trees, they have a way of gathering hanging moss, and little mushrooms often spring up from their toes. Most have two eyes. Some have only one, right in the middle of their foreheads. Trolls are hairy all over, except for their faces, and have absolutely enormous noses—so enormous, in fact, that trees sometimes sprout from them.

One forest troll was so huge, they say, that when he lay down, his head was in Sweden, and his feet were in the province of Lund near Finland. It was this same troll who once was so frightened by a thunderstorm that he ran over the mountains from Sweden into Norway. His footprints are still quite easy to see. One is Mjösa, the largest lake in Norway, and the other is Vänern, the largest lake in Sweden. So you see, forest trolls can get ridiculously big!

But when a forest troll baby is born, he is really rather small, only about three to four feet long. You can usually guess his age by the length of his tail, which he will use as a fishing line, handkerchief or lasso (or anything else it comes in handy for). But as he grows older, his tail grows shorter, and when it finally disappears he knows he is an adult.

Now lake troll babies have no tails, so it's harder to guess their age. Young or old, all lake trolls have webbed feet, for though you may see them walking on land, they really prefer to live under the water. Their heads are huge, their bodies are small, and their hair is long and flowing like seaweed.

They are quiet trolls. In Norway they are all called *Nökken* or *Nökkina*, and are known as the protectors of all the lakes. Deep under the surface they play with the fish and watch for any children who might fall in. So if you were to stand by Lake Sperillen as the moon was rising, you might see something begin to ripple the moonlight on the water. Then slowly the golden waves would part, and the great head of Nökken would rise to see if you needed help.

River trolls like to doze under wooden bridges. Here the waters lie still, forming quiet pools where, on hot summer days, trolls and fish love to nap. Now you might have read about one such troll who was very annoyed by the Billy Goats Gruff. If you did, then you might have the notion that trolls are very bad-tempered. But imagine yourself napping peacefully in a pool, only to have three goats come clattering across your bridge! The billy goats shock the bridge so hard that dust poured into the river, waking the old troll up and making him sneeze. His sneezing churned the water, and the water tossed the fish until they begged the old troll for help. Well, the thought of eating a goat tied his stomach in knots, but the troll *said* that's what he'd do just to scare the goats away.

So if you were to wander along the River Vågå, before it tumbles down into the canyon, you might stop quietly by the old wooden bridge. Perhaps you would see a shadow or hear a soft snoring.

Further along, you might also find small creeks entering the Vågå, making little waterfalls over the rocks. Here is the home of the water ouzel or "dipper." In Norwegian, this little bird's name is *fosekallen*, which means "old man of the waterfall"—for he is really a troll!

If you were to stop and sit down by one of these waterfalls, chances are you'd soon spot an ouzel. Then if you waited, watching him quietly, you might see him fly straight into the waterfall. You'd have to breathe ever so gently and listen

carefully, and you might catch a hint of music. For when a fosekallen flies under the waterfall, he turns into a troll about two feet tall. Then he takes out his violin and, holding it upside down to keep out the water, he plays the tunes of all he hears.

Mountain trolls are the most famous, of course, mostly because of their thunderous dance. A boy named Peer Gynt once learned their music and later taught it to a man named Grieg. Then Grieg set all Peer's adventures to that music, and from that the whole world learned about mountain trolls.

Mountain trolls are very hard to see, for they are as massive and craggy as the mountains themselves and their bodies are covered with mosses and lichen. It would be very easy to sit on a sleeping mountain troll, thinking it was just a pile of boulders. But when they move, it's a different story! Loud as thunder their muscles rumble, and their joints are always popping and groaning. When they cry their tears clatter down like hailstones, and the sound of their laughter is like the noise of a rockslide. They are also the most likely of all the trolls to turn into stone, for they have a habit of oversleeping in the sun. Still, for all their noise and clumsy ways, mountain trolls are the most bashful of all.

No matter where they live, trolls are quite friendly. There are sea trolls and barn trolls, house trolls, hill trolls, and some trolls nearly as old as the earth itself. For unless they have accidents or stay too long in the sun, trolls go right on living forever.

And so now you know a little about trolls. But let's get back to Lake Sperillen, where it is the sixteenth of May and the animals are gathering!

The Sixteenth of May

The sixteenth of May is a day of peace, even among the enemies of the forest. For though they may stalk each other the rest of the year, on this night they sense that it is safe to come together.

Now evening had come. Wolf, bear, fox and lynx moved down to the water's edge. The rabbits and other small animals sniffed the wind and soon joined the widening circle on the shore. Ears twitched. Tails flicked. Now the animals had to wait, for not until midnight would the real festivities begin.

As always, they would start with the dance of the cranes, and just as the sun spread his last rays over Troll Tinderne, a faint humming of wings was heard. Louder it grew, louder and louder, until the cranes flew in, silver-grey in the twilight, their heads softly crowned with bright red feathers. They landed in the animals' circle, ready to begin the dance.

Midnight came, but still they waited. The cranes stepped impatiently from one leg to the other. Where was Troll-Elgen? Where was their leader? For as long as any of the animals could remember, he had always opened their festivals on Lake Sperillen. They couldn't possibly begin without him! Surely he'd sensed the message on the wind!

Suddenly through the woods there came a great crashing. The ground trembled and branches cracked. Then there he stood, Troll-Elgen, the great bull elk. The animals say he is over seven hundred years old, and well he may be, for his fur is frosted white and all his joints are swollen with age. But this night, as always, he walked with dignity. His stride was firm, his head held high. His moss-covered antlers swept the tallest pines, and in respect all the animals stood on their hind legs.

Then, as is customary, Troll-Elgen was greeted by music. First came a soft thrumming from a hollow log occupied by a grouse. Then the capercaillie, with his red-ringed eyes, joined in, singing to all the animals the way he sings to his lady in the spring. Soon the bird's rich song set the wolves howling, the foxes crooning, and the bears and racoons humming along. The beavers drummed the ground with their broad, flat tails, and last of all the ptarmigans joined in. Now it was time for the dance of the cranes!

With long steps and wings lifted gracefully, the leader bent to pick up a stick. High in the air she tossed it, and another swooped and caught it in his beak. He threw it high and another caught it, then another and another, each taking the leader's place in the center of the circle. Faster and faster went the dance, and the music swelled with each toss of the stick.

When the cranes had finished, the animals thrummed the ground in applause. Now to the center came two arctic loons, black as midnight except for little white spots that spangled their feathers like tiny stars. Their strange cry rang out across Lake Sperillen and came echoing back like a crazy laugh. Then both birds ran down to the water's edge, swiftly, smoothly, without a sound. Silently they spun around and swiftly ran back. And had you stood watching the lake that night, you would have thought that tiny stars sped over its shores.

Now the animals would feast and sing! There by Lake Sperillen, they raised their voices, knowing their song would travel up the Vågå to the trolls.

High on Troll Tinderne the song was heard. Here the trolls from all over Norway were gathering. Shadows of every size and shape now moved in slowly around the flickering fire. You see, only once a year do all trolls come together, for they are generally shy and stick to their own trolldoms. But they wouldn't miss their Council for all the world! Trolls have a funny way of copying humans, especially when it comes to a celebration. Like their fellow Norwegians, they sing and dance and carry on until morning. At the moment, though, they were just curiously eyeing one another, knowing they would soon be dancing together for their homeland.

For comfort, some of the river trolls had brought along their bridges, and all the fosekallens had their fiddles. But at the moment the only music came from the lakeshore below. Up until now, the trolls had been listening and swaying, but suddenly each one turned his ears toward the forest. All movement stilled as they waited.

At last they heard it—heavy footsteps, rumbling like tree roots pulling loose from the soil, so loud that even the animals' music stopped. All eyes looked up. Then over the crest of Troll Tinderne he came, almost as tall as the trees themselves—Storegubben, the Master Troll of Norway!

Now to be honest, Storegubben is not much to look at. He has a bad overbite, a tremendous nose, and a face as gnarled as old hickory bark. His eyes glow as red as embers, but even these are not as strong and bright as once they were. Sometimes, because Storegubben is more than eleven hundred years old, those fiery eyes flicker out all together. This means the old forest troll has to stop whatever he's doing, pop them out, and blow on them to get them going again. Still, he is majestically tall, and this night his voice swelled among them like a storm.

"*Velkommen, Troll!*" he called in Norwegian. "Now the feast begins and we dance for Norway!"

Then how the animals' music swelled from down below! The fosekallens raised their fiddles and the river trolls bravely set aside their bridges. Gone was their shyness! Now they would dance! And soon all Norway was thundering with their steps. They jumped and hopped and kicked up their heels, laughing and leap-frogging, spinning round and round. Each swoosh of the forest trolls swelled like a wind in the trees, while the river trolls whooshed like the rush of wild water. Around them leapt the mountain trolls, thundering down so hard that lightning flashed out when their feet struck the ground. On and on they danced, until high on Troll Tinderne a storm seemed to rage, and down in the farmlands the children smiled to themselves.

Later mushrooms were munched, honey gulped, and berries gobbled by the bucketful. At last they collapsed, exhausted, around the fire.

This was the time when Storegubben always told a tale. Being the oldest and wisest of trolls, he knew a Council should always end with some thought. Tonight he would tell them about the Vikings, those brave Norwegian seamen who had discovered the New World.

Now it might seem a little funny to you that a great troll should talk of such tiny creatures as human beings. But then you have to remember that, being Norwegian, trolls are proud of their fellow countrymen, however small; and they like especially to hear about deeds that trolls themselves have never done. And so as his hands waved over the fire, Storegubben told of Leif Ericson and Eric the Red, who had voyaged to a far-off land called America. He told of Roald Amundsen, who discovered the South Pole, and of Fridtjof Nansen who crossed Greenland on skis.

"Ja, and for small folk, they were brave for sure," sighed a one-eyed troll, slightly smaller than Storegubben.

"Brave and a little crazy perhaps! They had such dreams in their heads, those Vikings!" chuckled Storegubben.

The one-eyed troll blinked. "Was ever a troll a Viking?" he asked.

The Master Troll just shook his head. "I think not. But one thing sure, it was a troll who told Eric the Red where he should go!"

"H-he did?" stuttered a fosekallen. "But if he knew so m-much, why didn't that t-troll go himself?"

"Ah," sighed Storegubben. "You know very well. Like a tree, a troll has deep roots in his homeland."

"Not me!" said the one-eyed troll, much to everyone's surprise. "I often dream of a day when I will travel across the ocean to the New World."

Like a whirlwind, a gasp swept round the fire.

Now this troll's name is Dovergubben, and like Storegubben he is of grandfather age. At the time, he was the leader of a small trolldom near Oslo that included eleven other trolls. And all of them, seeing the light of adventure in Dovergubben's eye, quickly gathered around him.

Storegubben raised one eyebrow. "Dovergubben," he said firmly, "you are old and you are wise. You know such dreams don't come from nowhere."

"Ah, maybe they come from the New World herself," sighed Dovergubben. "Lately a voice calls to me, *Come to America!*"

All the other trolls snickered into their shoulders.

"What did you say, Dovergubben?" asked Storegubben.

Dovergubben repeated it.

Storegubben stood up. "America, it is very far," he said, "but the wind tells me many Norwegians now live there."

"Then for sure a troll could make it too!" cried Dovergubben.

"Ja, but a troll, he is not human you know," warned Storegubben. "Trolls have no boats, no way for the crossing."

"But who needs boats? A troll could walk the North Sea! Wait 'til she's crusted over with ice! A troll could walk the whole Arctic Ocean!" argued Dovergubben.

Then a hundred voices rumbled round the fire. "No troll would want to leave his homeland! A troll in the New World? This troll is crazy! A troll belongs at home in his trolldom!"

But Storegubben raised his hand. "A trolldom," he said sternly, "is wherever its troll is."

With that everyone fell silent. Down below, the capercaillie began his haunting song again.

"My friends," said Storegubben with a glimmer of a smile, "tonight among us we have a Viking troll. Tonight such a light I see in Dovergubben's eye, it reminds me of only one other pair of eyes!"

"Whose eyes?" thundered several voices.

"A human's," murmered Storegubben.

"What human?" they demanded.

"Just a friend," replied Storegubben. "But Dovergubben, my friend! You forget! A troll can exist only in a land where he's believed in!"

For a moment Dovergubben's eye flickered out. Then it flared like a torch. "Ja," he said with a great smile. "And you yourself have just said that Norwegians—I mean human Norwegians—live in the New World. Surely they will believe in us!"

"Us?" echoed Dovergubben's eleven trolls. "You would take us too?"

"Why, what good would be a new trolldom with only one troll?" laughed Dovergubben. And he gave his wife, Grandmother Kjerringa, a hug. "Sure I will take you if you want to go."

"Wh-where Dovergubben goes, so g-go his trolls!" stuttered the group's little fosekallen bravely.

The ten others nodded. But Storegubben shook his head. "No troll makes such a choice in one night," he said. "Now we must sleep, and while we all dream, keep in mind these thoughts which now I will tell you. Sure though a troll's steps be half a field long, a trip of this sort could take up to a year. Arctic ice grows no berries, no honey, no seed. All food would have to be carried upon your backs. And sure though a troll's fur is thick and warm, never could it keep out the polar wind!"

Dovergubben's group shivered in the dark.

"And you might have to carry your babies as well," Storegubben went on. "And beware of the sun or you'll turn to stone!" He sighed sadly. "Ja, that is why Norway herself is so rocky. So sleep, my trolls! Dream! And tomorrow night we meet!"

Then all the trolls nodded. They would stay on Troll Tinderne one more night. After all, they were eager to know what would come of this.

Down below the animals had stopped their song, for a pale rim of light was outlining Troll Tinderne. The night of the sixteenth of May was over.

And had you been standing on the shore of Sperillen, you might have seen great shadows rise on the mountain. Then as you rubbed your eyes in the dawn, their shapes would have slowly faded into the trees.

Farvel

Now a funny thing happened as the trolls slept. For though they tried to keep in mind the words Storegubben had told them, all sorts of other sounds tickled their ears. Drums! Flutes! Singing and laughter! It was May seventeenth, and the people of Norway were celebrating!

At dusk they woke, their ears all atingle from the far-off music of marching bands. Ah, who can say how such things really work, but that music ignites all the dreams in a troll! Dovergubben's group had gone to sleep excited enough, but on waking they could barely contain themselves!

The other trolls watched with little grins. Soon Storegubben would arrive to set these trolls straight, to put an end to their outlandish plans! But where was he? Anxiously they peered around the forest. You see, the Master Troll has a way of sleeping late, and in fact sometimes oversleeps more than a year. Finally he will waken to recall he had a meeting with you.

This worried Dovergubben, and the more he worried, the more his eye bulged. Suddenly it popped out and went rolling down the mountain. Poor Grandmother Kjerringa! Down she trundled after it, while the other trolls chuckled to themselves. You see, at this time Kjerringa was seven hundred years old, and Dovergubben over nine hundred. This was hardly fitting behavior for two such old trolls, especially trolls who wanted to lead an expedition!

Well, the others in Dovergubben's group were no better. They were so anxious for the meeting with Storegubben that they had to do something to calm themselves down. So they began playing catch with the troll babies. (And by the way, if you ever babysit a troll baby, just remember this is the best way to keep him out of mischief.)

Being forest trolls, the parents Langemann and Nesa stationed themselves among the trees. You see, Langemann means "long man" and Nesa "the nose," so between them they could reach to the highest branches. First Langemann tossed Rumpungen, named for his little round rump. Then Nesa tossed Kalvehalen by her long curling calf's tail.

High over Troll Tinderne went the laughing troll babies, to be caught by two mountain trolls, Jotulen and Kari. They had stationed themselves high up on the boulders and now tossed the troll babies down to the river.

Here Fosekallen of the waterfall moved quickly aside. You see, forest troll babies are so much bigger than he that he gladly let the lake trolls take his place. Up they jumped, Nökken and his wife Nökkina, using their webbed feet to catch those falling furballs. Now their little son, Nökkungen, begged to join in, and this time three troll-tots went sailing through the trees.

"*O Himmel!* What's going on?" boomed a voice.

All the trolls looked up. It was Storegubben!

Well, even the other trolls blushed a little, for they had caught the spirit of the game and had been cheering from the sides. At the sound of the voice, Dovergubben again lost his eye, which sent Grandmother Kjerringa running, which set the other trolls laughing, which made everyone forget about the troll babies soaring overhead.

Storegubben stared. What had happened to his meeting? And what on earth were those things flying through the air? But trolls will be trolls, so when he realized they were giggling troll babies, he nimbly leapt up and tried to catch all three. Then how the other trolls laughed, for though the Master Troll did catch two, the third—little Nökkungen—landed on the great forest troll's head!

"K-keep him there, Storegubben! It will k-keep him out of mischief!" piped Fosekallen, much to the troll mother's dismay.

But Storegubben gently bowed down to Nökkina, who was now standing at his feet, wringing her hands.

"O, *mange takk*, Storegubben," she thanked him. She untangled her baby from the Master Troll's mossy hair. "By himself, my Nökkungen would have never gotten down."

Storegubben straightened up. "In just such a way did I once save a human, a young one who climbed me thinking I was a tree!"

"What young one?" asked all the trolls together.

But Storegubben only turned with a faint smile. "Come," he said. "Now we meet."

Once more the trolls clustered round the fire. Not just Dovergubben's group but all the trolls waited for the Master's words.

"We have slept many hours and dreamed many dreams. And in our ears has the wind been whispering its tales..." Storegubben stopped and raised his eyebrows. "What did it tell you of so grave a trip?"

The trolls blushed a little, recalling the flutes and drums of their dreams.

Finally Dovergubben spoke, all festivity drained from his face. "In my dreams did a voice speak of many dangers—of a beast with teeth much longer than swords, of a place where the wind cuts like a knife to your bone..."

"Ja, and what of you others?" questioned Storegubben.

Where moments before they had all been laughing, now Dovergubben's group looked grim indeed! For woven between the music and laughter of their sleep, they too had heard whispers and seen visions of danger. Each troll told of the lands of his dreams. Most often they were endless vistas of white.

"And would you still go?" questioned Storegubben.

Nesa and Nökkina cuddled their young ones close. For some reason everyone seemed to be looking at them.

"Ja," they murmured after a long time.

Then such a chorus of cheers rang from Troll Tinderne as has never been heard before or since.

"*Vidunderlig, Troll!*" cried Storegubben. "So! Now we have true Vikings among us!"

All the trolls clustered around Dovergubben's group, most to congratulate them, of course, but a few to tell them how crazy they were.

"But how shall we find our way?" asked Grandmother Kjerringa, who, as you will learn, is always the first to spot a problem.

"Simple, follow your noses!" declared Storegubben.

And of course he was right, for a troll's nose is very sensitive. Like a compass it can sense direction, and as long as the troll trusts it, he cannot go far wrong.

"Ja, but we could follow our noses forever," said Nesa. "Somewhere, someday, we surely must stop!"

"Ah," answered Storegubben, "now may you listen. For the wind is my friend, that you well know. All my life it's been whispering of places it's been to, and where it goes it tells in my dreams. It's been traveling since the world first began, picking up voices and blowing them around. Old voices, young voices, voices long ago . . . "

Then suddenly Storegubben stopped. He drew a long breath, as if he wanted to suck in the wind itself, so through his mouth it could speak its own words.

"But way back eleven hundred years," he continued, "I first heard it speak of a land to the west. Far over the ice and tundra and plains lies a land, so it's said, as fair as our Norway. The wind spoke of a mountain as lovely as Troll Tinderne and a lake as blue as the blue of Sperillen."

Then Dovergubben's group let out a sigh, for to find a land so like their homeland would indeed be a wonder.

"And will it be safe for trolls?" breathed Dovergubben.

"That I know not," said Storegubben. "But if you find it, and if it is safe for trolls, thenceforth shall it be called *Trollhaven!* It shall be known as a troll's home away from home, if ever any of you others choose to go traveling."

At this, all the other trolls' eyes grew so wide, they looked almost as excited as Dovergubben himself, and soon they fell to making plans. Together they decided it would be best if the expedition waited until October to set out. By then the northern ice would be forming and the trolls could walk on the frozen seas. In the meantime, that left June, July, August and September. Berries would be ripening and plants coming into season. It would take quite a harvest to stock up for the journey, but to Dovergubben's surprise, the rest of the trolls offered to stay on and help.

The month of May passed quickly and was soon gone. With it went thousands of geese, headed north. Huge herds of reindeer were now moving toward Lapland, and they stopped long enough to give milk for the ingrown toenail remedy.

"*Farvel!*" they called over their shoulders as they left. "You'll probably be gone before we return!"

Perhaps so! The preparations were moving right along. By June the troll men had made ten huge birch bark bags, and using the stems of the arctic cotton plant, the troll ladies had sewn the sides tightly together. By July many of the plants were ready to pluck, and by August the berries were ripening in the sun. Gooseberries, raspberries, blueberries, and tender bark went tumbling into the enormous bags. Roots, herbs, wild onions and seeds followed. The smallest bag was reserved for cloudberries, the favorite food of any troll. But these they vowed to eat only on special occasions.

By the end of September, all was ready. Chill winds now nipped the air and the wild geese were returning from their summer in the Arctic.

"How is it up there?" Grandmother Kjerringa called as they flew over.

"Wonderful!" they honked. "But it's growing cold!"

Then on the last day of September, Storegubben called all the trolls together. "Tomorrow we set out for Hardanger Fjord," he said, "and there shall we wait 'til the fjord ice forms. When it does and the North Sea is frozen over, we shall bid *farvel* to our troll expedition."

"But h-how," piped Fosekallen, "h-how will we know when we reach this land you spoke of?"

Storegubben smiled his mysterious smile. "Ahhh . . . a voice will come to you on the wind, like the voice that spoke in your dreams last May."

Then, more confused than comforted by these words, the trolls lay down for their last sleep on Troll Tinderne.

Early the next evening the wind blew cold, rattling the leaves around the sleeping trolls.

"Wake up," Dovergubben whispered to Grandmother Kjerringa. "It is time. We must get ready."

So while Kjerringa gathered the food supplies, Dovergubben went to rouse their companions. He shook Langemann, and woke Nesa by rustling the two mountain ash trees on her nose. Then he tickled their two troll babies. "Get up, Rumpungen," he whispered to a furry ball. "And you too, Kalvehalen!" he laughed, pulling her tail.

Next he went down and called across Lake Sperillen. "Nökken, Nökkina, Nökkungen!" echoed his voice.

Then, dragging their sleepy troll baby between them, the lake trolls waddled out on their flat webbed feet. Dovergubben was a bit concerned about those feet, because they were so much more tender than those of the others.

"Don't worry," said Nökkina bravely. "But maybe if Nesa would be so kind, Nökkungen could ride on her nose from time to time."

"Vidunderlig!" said Dovergubben, and he began climbing up toward the cave where all the mountain trolls were staying. Only the two named Jotulen and Kari would be going. Jotulen and his long-braided maiden friend were young trolls who had never left their families before. So, as Dovergubben climbed, tears began pelting his head, clattering off the cheeks of the older trolls above. In fact, had you been standing down below, you would have sworn it hailed on Troll Tinderne that evening.

Finally Dovergubben reached the cave. "If you keep that up much longer," he warned, "all Troll Tinderne will come tumbling down!" Then, after a few words with Jotulen and Kari, he headed for the waterfall. Just as he expected, there was Fosekallen, fiddling when he should have been getting ready!

This time, however, Fosekallen's song made Dovergubben stop and listen:

> *Where shall I be, when the cold winds blow?*
> *When the golden leaves wither and turn to snow?*
> *Off on the crust of a frozen sea,*
> *Eleven other trolls and me.*
> *O Norway, will you remember me?*
> *How I sang on your autumn wind, long ago?*
> *How I sang on your autumn wind?*

There among the scattered leaves, Dovergubben stood silent. All was golden in the dusk. This homeland he had known nine hundred years .... Gently the leaves dipped on the wind.

"She will remember," he called softly to Fosekallen. "And now you must come."

What a strange swaying there was in the forest that evening, as all the trolls of Norway made their way to Hardanger Fjord. Only the children peering from the farmhouse windows saw, and even then they were not sure if it was really trolls or just the trees stirring in the wind.

Before long, the trolls neared Oslo. They were very curious to look, but the noise hurt their ears, the bright lights hurt their eyes, and something in the air made them sneeze. So they skirted the city and kept to the country, and near dawn they arrived at Hardanger Fjord.

Here, where this long arm of the sea reaches deep into the land, ice was already forming and the Northern Lights were flickering. For almost two weeks the trolls waited on the shore. Animals gathered—reindeer, wolves, foxes, bears, and even the great Troll-Elgen himself—to guard the food bags day and night. Then on the thirteenth day of October, the ice was finally hard enough! Now, at the last dusk, there was much paw-shaking and nose-rubbing, and finally Storegubben gathered the twelve travelers around him.

"Now is all the world your home!" he said. "And so must you treat all lands like your own. For if kind and careful you are in the New World, perhaps she will come to accept your trolldom."

"And might others someday follow in their footsteps?" asked a troll who had been enviously eyeing Dovergubben.

"Perhaps," said Storegubben. "If they find the land, and if that land proves safe for trolls."

So many "if's" hung on the air. So many thoughts passed

between the eyes of the travelers and those who would stay behind. Silence filled the night. Slowly they put their arms round one another.

A squawk from little Kalvehalen broke the spell. She had sat so long, waiting for all the hugging to be done, that her tail had frozen fast to the ice! It took a good half-hour to chip her free—a delay typical of most any expedition.

Then at last the trolls set out on Hardanger Fjord. The wind was blowing up the surface ice, making it drift and swirl like ghosts among them. Again and again they turned to wave, as their friends grew small and faint in the distance.

Further and further along they trudged.

"Look," whispered Kalvehalen, looking back once more.

Everything behind them had vanished in the fog.

"Farvel, Norge!"

Now they were alone.

Islands on the Ice

Dovergubben was in the lead. Wisely, he had put the lake trolls right behind him, followed by Langemann, Nesa, Rumpungen and Kalvehalen. The forest troll family was followed by Fosekallen, who was followed by the mountain trolls, Jotulen and Kari. Grandmother Kjerringa took up the rear, for as the leader's wife, she wanted to make sure no one got lost.

From night into morning they trekked across the ice, and, still full of energy, they kept on going. This time of year is the dark season in the north country, so even at noon nobody worried about turning to stone.

On they went. Finally they reached the mouth of the fjord, and here they stepped onto the frozen North Sea. What a joy to walk so firmly on pack ice! Even Dovergubben could jump and still it would hold.

But they had walked long enough. Now it was time to rest for a while, and they stopped behind some huge crystal mounds. This ice towered at least forty feet high, and from the way it had been pushed up, layer by layer, the trolls guessed it was the work of the wind or current. It is known as "hummock," and if you ever camp in the Arctic, just remember the biggest mounds make wonderful windbreaks.

Here the trolls decided to make camp. How good the fruits and vegetables tasted! When they had finished eating, they stretched out on the birch bark bags. Their thick hair would keep them warm tonight, and, wiser now, Kalvehalen curled her tail on top of her belly. It had been a good first day.

When the trolls awoke the next morning, barely a shimmer of light came from the east. Overnight, frost crystals had settled in their fur in leaf shapes, flower shapes, and stars. They laughed to think how funny they would look back home.

"Just like a hairy *juletre*," rumbled the young bachelor Jotulen, shaking his crystal ornaments over Kari. The maiden troll giggled and tried to catch them as they fell.

Then, after a breakfast of roots and raspberries, they shouldered their sacks and set out once more. Trolls do not have any maps and, as you know, just follow their noses wherever they point; but had you yourself been on this expedition, you'd have known they were heading for Jan Mayen, the lone island in the wester ice of the Arctic.

All had been going along quite well until one day Nökkungen plopped down and began to cry. His tender webbed feet were scratched from the sea ice, and you can imagine how the salt made them sting. That was Nesa's cue. Much to her own troll babies' dismay, she set the little lake troll between the mountain ash trees on her nose. There he would ride happily for many days.

Darker and darker grew the Arctic. Days drifted. Weeks blew by. Blowing snow and mist often baffled the trolls. For here you can walk in circles without even knowing it, or slip

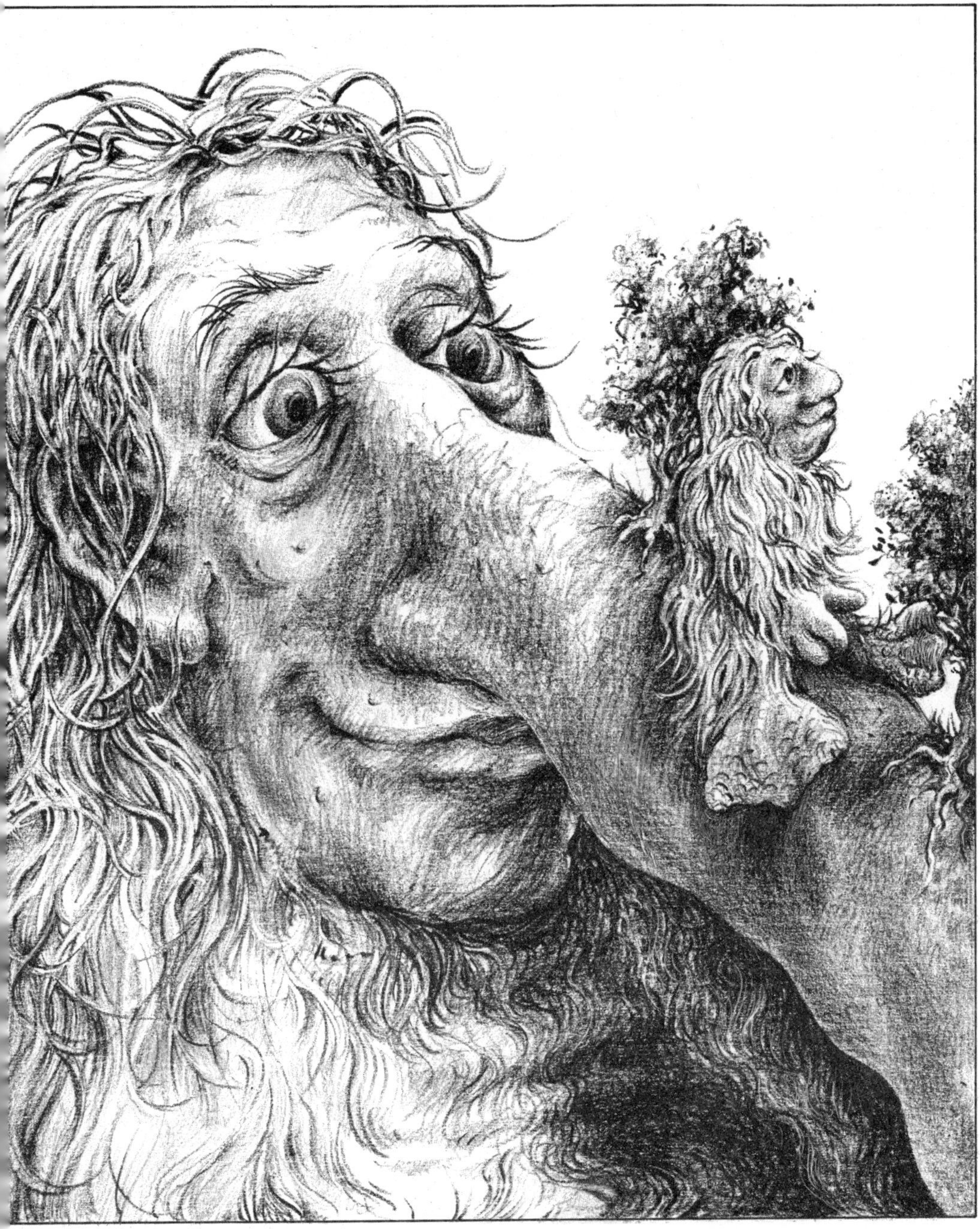

forever into the great open cracks called "leads."

Fosekallen was the first to sense the danger. "Let me turn into a bird!" he chirped. "I can fly above and scout the way!"

So, with the little ouzel flying above them for a guide, the trolls made their way across the frozen northern waters. Finally one day they spotted a peak in the distance.

"EN FJELL!" roared Jotulen, for being a mountain troll, he was naturally excited at the sight of anything rocky. "Come, Kari!" he called. "Run! Surely we can be there by supper!"

Dovergubben shook his head. "No. Two days more it will take," he cautioned.

But mountain trolls will learn only by experience, and Kari and Jotulen insisted they were right.

"Run on then," Dovergubben said. "But should your mountain grow no closer, turn around and come back here."

Off ran the mountain trolls, hand in hand across the ice.

"We will be waiting!" laughed Dovergubben, so sure he was that the mountain was much farther away than it looked.

While they waited, the trolls decided to add a treat to their food supplies. They set Kalvehalen and Rumpungen to fishing with their tails in an open lead, and in no time at all the forest troll babies had caught two huge codfish. Now trolls do not eat fish the same way humans do, so don't be surprised that Langemann let the cod freeze and then ground it into flaky fishmeal. This is a favorite food of trolls, except for lake trolls, of course. To them, fish are a troll's best friends, so naturally they don't want to eat them! In fact, lake trolls won't eat anything except what grows from the ground, a habit which other trolls find a bit tedious.

It was almost a whole day later when Jotulen and Kari reappeared, slumped together like tired boulders. "I would swear that mountain ran away from us!" panted Jotulen. But how glad he was to see the meal that was waiting! Roots, raspberries, and thick, rich fishmeal!

Dovergubben had been right. Islands on ice can play tricks on your eyes, and it was two more days before they reached Jan Mayen and its tallest mountain, which is called Berenberg.

Finally they set foot on land. They were a little sad that no one was there to greet them, and as they explored they were astonished to find very little snow.

Suddenly foxes began scampering out of nowhere, one pack blue and the other white. They eyed the strangers with curiosity.

"Trolls are we!" said Dovergubben's group, speaking in the manner of the animals. "Might we rest on your land?"

"It's about time we had some company," the foxes yipped. "And in summer thousands of seals will come join us!"

"Come summer, I doubt we'll be here," chuckled Dovergubben. "But at least we shall stay 'til our feet are rested."

Then the foxes led them to a place called Eggöya. "Many years ago a volcano erupted here," explained a fox. "See those big cracks where the steam seeps up? Nothing better for weary paws!"

Gratefully the trolls sat down and curled and uncurled their toes over the moist heat. Before they knew it, they were asleep, and to the foxes' surprise, they didn't move for two days.

Early the third morning the troll babies awoke to hear

strange noises coming from Tåkeheimen, a mountain whose name means "home of the fog."

"Do you suppose it's another volcano?" squealed Nökkungen.

Rumpungen listened. Sure enough, a great thunder echoed on the foggy mountain, and a little steam poofed up now and again. The troll babies huddled together. What was going on under that fog? Was Tåkeheimen going to explode? Suddenly the whole mountain seemed to shiver. Then, SWOOSH, an icy blast blew the fog away, and lo and behold! there on the top were the mountain trolls.

"What are you doing up there?" called the troll babies.

"Why, we gather saxifrage!" called Kari, scrambling to her feet. Then she and Jotulen ran down the mountain with armfuls of the wild purple herb.

The rest of the group were delighted to see the saxifrage. Though no human in his right mind would eat it, its dainty flowers are a favorite breakfast of trolls. They ate what the mountain trolls had gathered, then spent all day gathering more for their food bags.

"A long way have we come," said Dovergubben the next evening, "and foolish would we be to rush off so soon. These dark days are perfect for trolls. Let's stay here and gather strength for a while, for my nose tells me the next island is far away!"

The foxes were delighted that the trolls would stay, and each day took them exploring around the island. Only Jotulen and Kari stayed behind. For some reason, they were growing very fond of Tåkeheimen.

Now on Jan Mayen Island there are no trees, and the wind

sometimes blows two hundred miles an hour. This proved a bit hard on the troll babies, and one day such a blast almost blew them away. Fortunately, Rumpungen and Kalvehalen managed to wrap their tails around rocks. But not little Nökkungen! Away he went, sailing high over Tåkeheimen. The other trolls gasped! The lake troll baby was headed back to Norway!

"Help!" they cried helplessly at one another.

Then, high on the mountain top, two figures popped up! Just in time, they grabbed Nökkungen's webbed feet as he went whirling over their heads. Ah, thank heaven mountain trolls can't resist mountains! Up the slope ran all the trolls, to thank Jotulen and Kari for saving the lake troll baby.

In the days that followed, the trolls worried about Nökkungen, for the wind would even blow him off Nesa's nose. Finally the foxes had an idea. They led the group to a protected part of the island, where the lake trolls could swim in a freshwater lagoon. Here also was an old weather station.

"I once heard an explorer call it *Revesmuget*," said a fox, pointing to a little cabin where Nökkungen could stay.

"Ah, 'alley of the fox,'" Dovergubben translated with a laugh. "Your explorer must surely have been a Norwegian!"

And so the trolls' stay on Jan Mayen turned out happily after all. With saxifrage in their bellies each morning and the Northern Lights shimmering over them each night, they found it hard to think of leaving.

But by mid-November their food bags were filled to bulging again, and a far-off voice seemed to call on the wind.

The foxes heard it too, and guessed what it meant.

"Farvel!" the trolls called to them one morning, and

turned once more to follow their noses.

Dovergubben's nose had been right, for where they now headed was far away, over six hundred miles to the island of Spitsbergen. Of course, such a trek might seem terrible to you if you try to envision such vast acres of white. But for the trolls, every day was an adventure. Among the swirling mists they imagined dragon ships and Vikings battling through the fog. One day, however, something came through the fog which was definitely not imagined!

At first only Kalvehalen saw it. It was big and white and fluffy as a cloud. "A cloud baby!" she laughed, running toward it down the ice.

But suddenly the cloud flashed wild eyes and bared the sharpest teeth the little troll had ever seen!

Kalvehalen squealed and whirled around, but her long tail flew out and snagged on the screw ice. Nanook, the great Master Bear of the Arctic, was running right at her!

Far down the ice, the other trolls ignored the squeals. You see, by then they had learned not to be fooled by the screw ice. These great formations which the current twists up can sound like almost anything—a cannon firing, a dog barking, even a frightened troll baby crying!

"That crazy screw ice!" laughed Nesa, glancing around. "It sounds like my Kalvehalen!"

Kalvehalen! Where was she? In a flash, Nesa was racing down the ice! SMACK! she slapped Nanook with her great long nose! Then she swung that bear so hard and so high, he landed between two stars of the Big Dipper.

Now as the trolls continued on, other troubles beset them. Nökkungen still had sore feet and Nesa's nose had begun to bend with his weight. Her two mountain ash trees stood stripped of their berries, for the little lake troll had eaten every last one. Well, this set her nose out of joint even more! Then Grandmother Kjerringa started having problems too. Her ingrown toenails hurt worse every day, and the last drop of reindeer milk was already gone. All she could do was hobble slowly behind the others.

"Tired, *min elskede!*" Dovergubben asked her tenderly one day.

"Ah, no!" she lied. "Quite fine am I!"

Dovergubben looked down at her puffy purple toes.

"So you try to be brave and tell no one you hurt. What will become of you?" he asked.

Finally Kjerringa had to admit how hard the trek had become for her. They were all better off as a result. They soon found comfort in caring for the grandmother troll, and strength in helping her carry her load. Yet it was a hard journey! Now even their fur could not keep out the cold, and sometimes the wind whipped so hard across the ice, all they could do was huddle and sing to keep warm. Often around the fire those nights, their songs were lonely and longed for home:

> *Here we crouch where the cold winds blow.*
> *Have the golden leaves withered*
> *And turned to snow?*
> *Off on the crust of a frozen sea,*
> *Twelve forgotten trolls are we.*
> *O Norway, do you remember me?*
> *How I sang on your autumn wind, long ago?*
> *How I sang on your autumn wind?*

Now they had to go very slowly, for all the troll ladies' toes grew steadily worse. Often Rumpungen and Kalvehalen grew so tired, the adults had no choice but to drag them by their tails.

Only the mountain trolls felt no pain. Day after day they laughed and sang, running hand in hand across the ice. Their crazy songs and silly jokes seemed to make the journey brighter. Even Nesa finally had to smile, beneath her drooping nose.

Then at last—at long last—they saw something shining in the distance. By your map you would have recognized it: Spitsbergen, or *Svalbard* as it's sometimes called.

It was mid-December when they finally set foot on the foreland. Their feet were scabby, their backs ached, and all three troll ladies were crippled with ingrown toenails. Fosekallen's wings drooped like withered leaves, and when he turned into a troll, his arms were no better.

Shelter and sleep were all they could think of.

"But what can we build with?" groaned Grandmother Kjerringa, who was always the first to spot a problem. And as the trolls looked around the windswept island, they saw that she was right. There was driftwood scattered about, but not a single tree could they see.

"Well, couldn't we use the driftwood?" Nesa asked. She poked at a pile with her nose, and as she did, out came several scrawny lemmings. They stood looking wide-eyed at the trolls.

"Might we borrow some of your wood?" Langemann asked them.

But the lemmings neither spoke nor moved. They only

stood staring with their mournful eyes. "I guess they won't mind," Langemann said at last. Wearily then, the trolls began heaping up a shelter, stuffing the cracks with sod to keep out the wind. Finally like a towering heap of tangled elkhorn it stood, and the twelve aching trolls bent and crept in.

    A stranger sight you could not imagine! And had you been watching with the lemmings that night, you might have had to explain to them about trolls. For never had they seen such miserable creatures, and they asked themselves why such creatures should want to be *here*.

God Jul

Now, after a long sleep—and who could tell how long in that land of darkness?—the troll men woke so stiff and sore, they decided to make a restful day of it. But not Jotulen! He had too much energy for that! "See you tonight," he whispered softly, so as not to wake the troll ladies and babies. Then off he went to get reindeer milk, for he had seen a few tracks heading north.

"We'd *better* see him tonight," whispered Langemann to Dovergubben. He looked anxiously at the troll ladies' toes. "Should frostbite set in before he returns, we won't be leaving this island 'til spring."

Langemann and Dovergubben crept quietly out of the shelter. Surely there must be something on this island to protect a traveler from the bitter cold! Finding nothing among the rocks or along the barren shoreline, they headed inland. Finally, in a sheltered spot, they spied a patch of arctic cotton—the very same plant that grew back home!

The two trolls fell to their knees, and in no time they had armloads of the downy white fluff. Back to the driftwood shelter they hurried, and there they tucked the arctic cotton all around the troll ladies' feet.

"That should do it," Langemann sighed. "Now the warmth should stay in and keep the cold out." He tucked a little more under Nesa's feet, for as any expeditioner soon learns, good insulation is important, especially underneath!

No one had wakened, not even the troll babies. Wearily Langemann and Dovergubben lay back down. All day long they slept in the hut, and after many hours Jotulen returned. How the lady trolls beamed when they saw him! Not only had he brought birch sap and reindeer milk, but also great tufts of reindeer hair. "They rub it off when they scratch against the birch trees," Jotulen chuckled. "And they told me it makes wonderful lining for moccasins."

Then in an ice-stiffened birch bark bag, Dovergubben mixed the only known remedy for ingrown troll toenails. How soothing it was! Sloshing their feet around in the mixture, the troll ladies set about shaping moccasins from the arctic cotton. With the tough stems, the troll men sewed them together, and the troll babies stuffed them with the reindeer hair.

They tried them on. Like magic shoes, these soft new slippers suddenly made them want to dance! Who cared about sore feet? Up they jumped, and in a minute were leaping and whirling to Fosekallen's fiddle!

The hut swayed with music. It twinkled with light. But outside, the sad-eyed lemmings stood grim. Couldn't these trolls see how bitter this land was? Why bring such melody? Why bring such song?

Now it was only a few days before Christmas, and just like humans, the trolls were starting to get itchy. They dreamed of the celebrations back home in Norway, and wondered where they would ever find a Yule tree.

Again the trolls glanced around the barren island. Wasn't there anything they could use? Then Langemann picked up a stick of driftwood. "Ja," he declared, "and if it's good enough for shelter, it's good enough for a *juletre!*" And with that he began tangling smaller pieces into larger ones until, sure enough, he had made a sort of tree shape.

"And here is some green!" Nökkina laughed as she started twisting seaweed—the only green thing to be found—around the branches of the "tree." The others joined in, weaving the seaweed round and round the bottom, while the troll babies scrambled with it up to the very top.

"Ja, but what of ornaments?" asked Grandmother Kjerringa, who could always think of one more problem.

But that was no problem at all. For the next few days the troll babies combed the island, finding little blue mussels, purple periwinkles, and a crusty old starfish to go on top. Then on Christmas Eve the trolls decorated their tree, for in Norway that is when the celebration begins.

"*God jul! God jul!*" they called to one another when it was finished.

And now, like great curtains, the Northern Lights danced around them, shimmering red and green and blue. Dovergubben found a flint and struck a fire. Then one by one the trolls joined hands and, as is the custom, slowly circled their juletre. Later they sang and feasted on cloudberries that they had been saving all the way from Norway.

Now for the gifts! *Gifts?* They looked at each other in surprise. Why, how could it be a good Yule without any gifts?

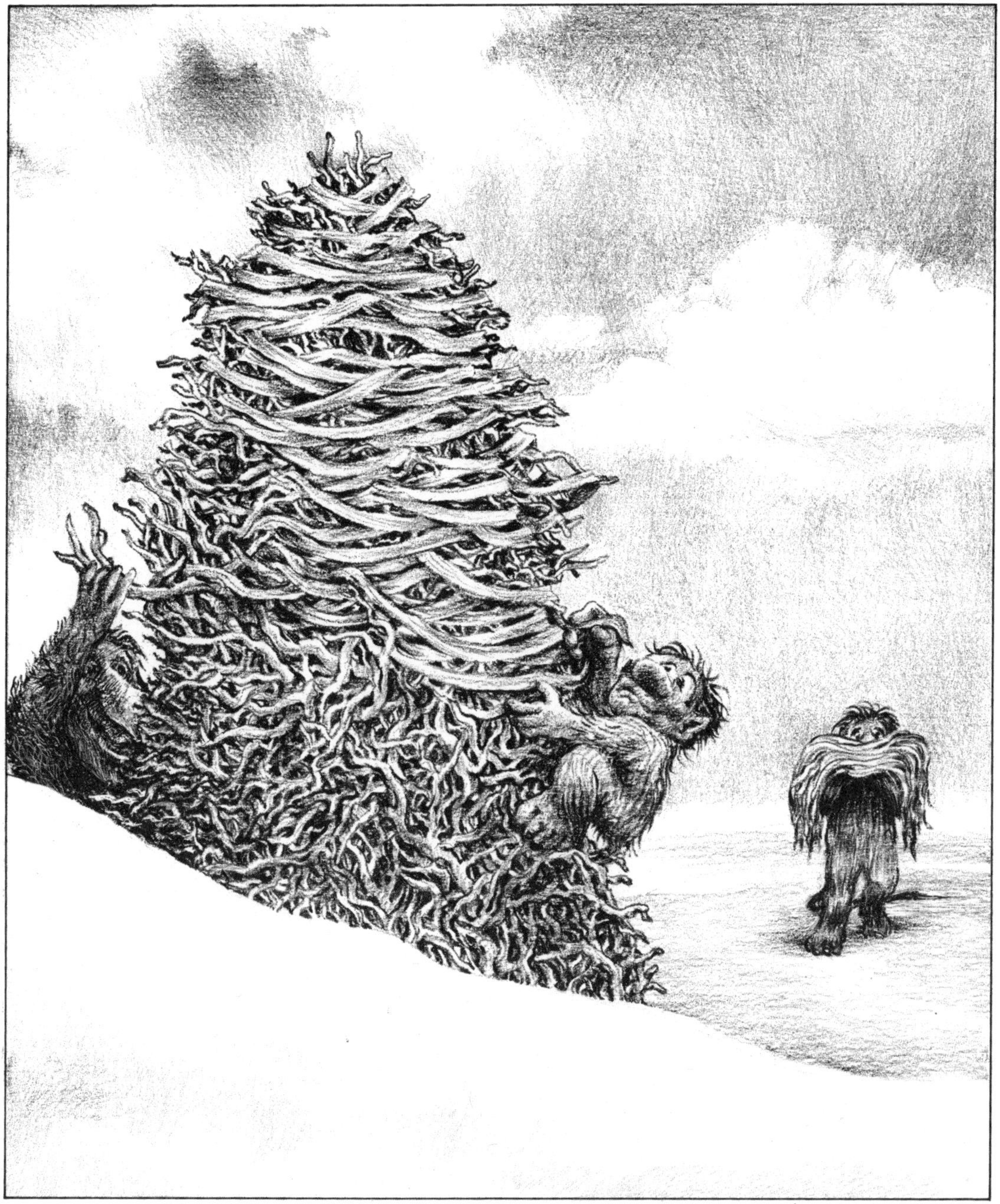

Again they glanced around the wasteland. Nothing, nothing at all! Nothing, that is, except those sad-eyed lemmings who were forever staring but never spoke. *They* certainly wouldn't be very merry gifts for anyone!

"Well, a troll can always give thanks!" said Nesa.

So that's exactly what they did! They thanked each other one by one, and then turned silently to the starry night. All was still.

They stood a long time in the darkness. Where would they be a year from now? Making a new trolldom across the sea? Celebrating their Trollhaven on Christmas Eve? Or would they all be wandering still, in search of the place the wind spoke of?

Then, and no one could say just when it started, it seemed they heard music, like little bells or chimes ringing in the night. Was it their ears, or was it really music? They listened. No, not bells, but more like voices singing, so far away that there was no telling if they were human, animal, or troll.

No one dared speak, but as they listened, a soft peace settled over them all.

"Wh-what is it?" whispered Fosekallen.

"I don't know," answered Dovergubben quietly. "Some things perhaps a troll will never know."

And perhaps they wouldn't. But deep in their dreams, the music echoed on and on, on beyond space, on beyond time, with its mysterious message from who knew where . . .

The day after Christmas, Dovergubben was bending over gathering lichen. He had just lost his eye when he heard someone step up to him. That someone said nothing, but Dovergubben could tell who it was just by the sound of cracking knuckles and creaking joints. "Well, what is it, Jotulen?" he asked, as he popped his eye back in.

The young bachelor blushed and pretended to look at the sky.

"Speak up, speak up!" Dovergubben urged.

Jotulen took a very deep breath. In fact, he must have sucked in half the air on Spitsbergen, for the driftwood hut swayed dangerously in the distance.

"Urrr... grmmm..." he rumbled. "I was, um, wondering if you might... I mean, if you could... I, uh... Dovergubben, would you do a troll wedding?"

Well, Dovergubben was so surprised, his eye popped right out again. Again he had to search for it, again polish it, and again pop it back in place. Then he asked Jotulen if he would mind repeating himself.

Jotulen stammered out his request once more.

"But you don't need *my* say-so!" Dovergubben reminded him. (You see, trolls seldom have weddings; they generally just take up living together.)

"Is it so important?" Dovergubben asked.

Jotulen blushed again. "I-I just thought a ceremony might make it a little more... well... *solid*," he mumbled.

"Solid?" laughed Dovergubben. "Ja, you're a mountain troll to the core!" And then, because no troll can pass up a chance for a party, Dovergubben agreed to perform a "solidification" on New Year's Eve.

Then what merriment there was! For even though the trolls weren't the least surprised that Jotulen and Kari wanted to live together, they were delighted that there was to be another celebration!

Of course, as you might expect, the troll ladies immediately started bustling about. Poor Jotulen! He did not know what to do! Everywhere he went, he seemed to be in the way, and at every turn he stumbled over his big mountain feet.

Finally Grandmother Kjerringa made a suggestion. "Dovergubben," she said, "might you take Jotulen away for a few days? Then maybe we can get some preparing done!"

And so it was that Dovergubben, Langemann, Nökken and Fosekallen decided to take the bridegroom on a side trip. You see, they had heard the sad-eyed lemmings whisper a grim tale of a place called Bear Island. There, from what they could make of the whispers, lived a horse that had been stranded by an expedition. Since nothing grew on the island for the horse to eat, he'd finally learned to run out to sea to catch seals. And so, much against his gentler nature, the abandoned animal had become a meat-eater.

Now the trolls didn't like the idea of such a killer, and they thought he just might change his ways if they offered to take him along on their journey. Off they set, taking great strides across the ice, and before long they arrived on Bear Island.

There was no sign of a horse along the shore. But it was late, so they set up camp for the night and agreed to look for him in the morning.

But morning came and went, and still no horse. For two days they searched the tiny island, but not a horse hair nor hoof print nor dropping could they find. Then, on the third morning, they woke to strange noises. Thousands of birds were flocking the sky and coming to rest on a mountain.

"M-maybe they can t-tell us where the horse lives," piped Fosekallen. With a flurry, he fluttered himself into a bird and was headed for the lofty peak. Quickly, the others scrambled up after him.

Now the trolls did not know it, but this is Bird Mountain, the home of thousands and thousands of fulmars. In Norway they call this bird *havhest*, which means "horse of the sea." In summer, when the sea thaws, the fulmar flies so low over the waves that he seems to be riding on them. He also has a special way of protecting himself. No matter who the intruder might be—fox, human, or even a troll—the fulmar will spit a bright red liquid.

But knowing none of this, the trolls eagerly bounded up Bird Mountain, and in no time Jotulen was bending over a nest.

"*God morgen!*" he greeted. "Do you happen to know a meat-eating . . . ?"

"FSSSsssssst!" Out shot the spit! It hit Jotulen right in the eyes, and before the others could catch him, such a crashing there was you would have thought all of Bird Mountain was coming down. When the others finally reached him at the bottom, Jotulen was a mountain of bruises, and he couldn't see a thing because of the spit.

"I'm th-thinking we should head h-home," said Fosekallen that evening as they sat around the fire. "F-for who knows if we will ever f-find that horse?"

"Ja, perhaps," Dovergubben nodded. "Perhaps another expedition found him, and even now he's home in his barn eating hay."

Well, at least it was comforting to think so, and the next

morning they headed back for Spitsbergen. The trip was understandably slow, what with guiding that battered and blinded bridegroom between them. But by the time they arrived, Jotulen could see again. For sure, he had no trouble spotting Kari right away!

"What was that great thunder we heard?" she asked when all the nose-rubbing was done.

"Why, don't you know?" laughed Fosekallen. "Th-that's how your bridegroom says good morning!"

But the trip had served its true purpose: with Jotulen away, the lady trolls had been able to get everything ready for the wedding. The travelers had returned on the last day of the old year, and on the first eve of the new, Jotulen and Kari would be united.

The troll ladies had spent a good part of their time making a surprise for the bride-to-be, and on the morning of her wedding, Kari tried it on for the first time. It was a sort of veil made entirely from seaweed that Nökkungen and Nökkina had gathered from beneath the ice. Now if you think seaweed is only green, you would have looked twice at Kari's veil. It was all shades of blue, green, and yellow, and fastened with lustrous red kelp.

Of course a wedding is no wedding without music, so while Kari was trying on her veil, Langemann made a harp from a piece of driftwood and strung it with strands of arctic cotton. Meanwhile the troll babies had gathered blue mussels and tied a stone in each one to make a bell. Now, ringing their bells, they raced up and down the island, while at the foot of the glacier, Fosekallen tuned his fiddle.

At last the hour came. The Northern Lights began to

shimmer and the moon rose, setting the snowfield aglisten. For the first time in history, two trolls would be united away from home, and as Dovergubben led the procession to Lungyer Glacier, Grandmother Kjerringa frequently had to blow her nose.

Behind them came Kari in her veil of seaweed, followed by Langeman playing his harp. Nesa had decorated her trees for the occasion, and as always, Nökkungen rode between them. Behind them came Jotulen, and for the first time in years the bashful fellow had a broad smile on his face. Not that he had been unhappy before; but mountain trolls tend to have rather bad teeth, which makes them a little shy about smiling. Anyway, all that was forgotten now.

Following Jotulen came Nökken and Nökkina, followed by the troll babies ringing their bells. Last of all came Fosekallen, gently playing the song of the waterfall.

Finally they reached the glacier. Here the trolls formed a circle, with Jotulen and Kari in the middle. Dovergubben was not much for words, so the solidification was quite brief.

"Jotulen and Kari," said the ancient troll, "far are you now from the land you call home. Ja, but the real home is the home you make in your hearts. Go where you will, you will always have each other; and the wider your love, the wider will grow your home, 'til all creatures become your family."

Then as Jotulen and Kari held hands, Dovergubben pronounced them troll and troll.

Stillness fell over the Arctic, broken only by the cracking of ice.

But weddings are for celebrating, and troll weddings are no exception. In no time they were dancing round and round.

Ever frowning, the lemmings looked on. Could these be the same miserable creatures who had staggered onto Spitsbergen only two weeks before? What did they think life was all about, anyway?

Maybe you would have answered them, but then again, maybe not. For if you had told them where the trolls were headed, they might well have started muttering, "More misery ahead!"

All an expedition needs is a pessimist!

The lemmings were right about one thing, though. The route ahead would be treacherous indeed.

Ah, but tomorrow the trolls would face troubles enough. Tonight let's leave them dancing beneath the stars!

The Leader in the Lead

The next morning the wind blew harsh and bitter. At least to the trolls it *felt* like morning, for you're never quite sure in that land of darkness. Great icebergs were barely visible on the horizon, and the trolls sniffed the wind to get a sense of direction.

Yes, it was time to move on. All the troll ladies had outgrown their ingrown toenails, and the food bags sat waiting as before. So, once more in a line, they moved out onto the frozen sea, stopping for a moment to look back at their driftwood hut. Who knew where they would be stopping next?

Crouched in the hut, the sad-eyed lemmings watched them go. These strangers who had come out of nowhere now were vanishing into nowhere. The lemmings sniffed for the music, for a trace of song. Perhaps it would all come back again tonight. They waited. Perhaps they wait still. . . .

Meanwhile, half a mile out, an ice fog was setting in, turning the trolls' hair to stiff crystal. Through the day it grew steadily worse. "We might as well be blocks of ice," grumbled Jotulen, clanking against Kari.

The next day was no better, nor the next, nor the next. The fog closed in, growing thicker and thicker until they could barely see their own noses. Then suddenly a lead would gape open before them and they would have to take a long detour around it. What a vicious maze it was! If only they could tell where the next lead lay!

Then one day, after walking around the biggest lead yet, Grandmother Kjerringa laughed and pointed to the sky. "A map!" she shouted. "A map in the sky!"

Surely Kjerringa had lost her mind! Of course, ice fog would be hard on anyone's grandmother.

But when they looked where she pointed, they did notice something. A great dark patch shone black against the white.

"You see? It's the same size and shape as this lead!" Kjerringa cried. "A reflection! Like a mirror in the sky!"

And so it was. The grandmother troll had discovered the secret of the sky map! Soon they found that by watching for these patches in the sky, they could tell exactly where the next lead lay, and so avoid taking all those detours.

On they trudged, week after week, avoiding the leads—but going where? Sometimes the fog closed in so thick there was no way of telling up from down. Only if you can imagine walking around inside a snowball will you know how the trolls were beginning to feel. They would stand dizzily, sniffing the wind, and then suddenly lose their balance and topple over. Now another fear began to grip them. What if they were headed backward? Or worse yet, what if they were walking in one continuous circle?

Then one day an unforeseen lead gaped open before them. In it was an enormous head, and as it rose from the water, so did two long teeth—teeth much longer than any they had ever seen, except... except.... Forgotten memories flashed through their minds: *In my dreams did a voice speak of many dangers, of a beast with teeth much longer than swords...*

They leapt back.

It swam toward them.

Then, as it reached the ice's edge, it flung back its head and sank those great teeth in! Its eyes rolled upward.

"I like him!" shouted Nökkungen. "He wants to play!"

And before Nökkina could stop him, the little lake troll had jumped into the lead.

"Come back!" screamed Nökkina.

The beast let go of the ice and began to turn. Nökkina reached frantically for her baby.

"Wait," whispered Nökken, drawing her back. "Perhaps our little Nökkungen is right."

Now if you had seen Nökkungen's eyes at the moment, you might have noticed a flicker of fear. The beast was swimming steadily toward him, and this strange salty water made the troll baby sneeze. Bubbles frothed around him. He gasped and sputtered. But had you been watching the eyes of the stranger, you'd have seen how they began to crinkle at the edges. Suddenly came the funniest guffaw the trolls had ever heard.

What a heave of relief came from the group on the ice! Then down in the water the two heads met. Bump! went their noses. Bump-brush to the right. Bump-brush to the left. A sure sign of friendship in the Arctic!

Nökkungen was quick to introduce himself. "God dag!"

he said with a smile. "I am called Nökkungen!"

"And I am called nothing," the animal shrugged. "Or if I once had a name, I've forgotten it now."

"I think in Norway they call him *hvalross*!" shouted Dovergubben from up on the ice.

"Then I'll call you Vally," Nökkungen declared. "But what are these called?" he asked, grabbing the great teeth.

"Why, tusks!" said Vally. "How else should I scrape shellfish from the sea?" With that he dove down and came right back up with a clam, which he crunched and swallowed, shell and all.

"They're also my defense against Nanook," he continued. "I'm the only animal on the pack ice that rascal doesn't bother!"

"Well, he's no bother now!" Nökkungen laughed. "For Rumpungen's mother threw him up among the stars!"

Vally stared at the trolls. "But what are *you*?" he asked. "Never before have I seen such a group! Once I saw some people go down in a ship. Are you people?"

The trolls laughed. To think trolls could be mistaken for humans! "Trolls we are!" announced Dovergubben. "On an expedition to the New World!"

"But you're so many shapes and sizes!" Vally exclaimed.

"And so is the land from which we come," Nökkungen said. "You see, I'm a lake troll, and those others with webbed feet like mine, those are my parents. The lumpy ones to their right are mountain trolls, and the others are forest trolls."

"Lakes, mountains, forests," mused Vally, munching his mustache. Then he shook his head. "The only thing slightly familiar to me is that little bird on the great one's shoulder."

"But he too is a troll!" laughed Nökkungen.

Fosekallen fluttered his feathers. In a second, there he stood on Dovergubben's shoulder, the troll of the waterfall, fiddle and all! With a flourish, he drew his bow and began to play—not the song of the waterfall this time, but an old Norwegian *slott*, the song the mountain folk dance to in the highlands. Faster and faster he fiddled, until Vally's head began to sway to and fro.

"Such a fine sense of rhythm he has!" sang Fosekallen.

Then Vally could resist no more. Deep under the waves he dove, heaving and humping up and down in a dance few humans ever see. Now Nökkungen joined in by straddling Vally's shoulders, and together the two went plunging through the lead. Soon foot-tapping started up on the ice, then swaying, then swirling, then leaping about.

For weeks the trolls had known nothing but fear. Now they kicked up their heels as never before! Never had they seen Dovergubben so gay! In fact, Fosekallen had to grab hold of Dovergubben's hair to keep from bouncing right off his shoulder.

That did it! The grab so startled Dovergubben, he threw back his head and lost his eye. Groping, he swooped to pick it up, missed, and fell headlong into the lead!

The others howled with laughter.

"L-look!" sputtered Fosekallen. "Our l-leader's in the lead!"

You see, they knew that though a forest troll can't swim, his hair will buoy him up and keep him afloat. There like a hairy log Dovergubben floated, with his hand over his eyehole to keep out the water.

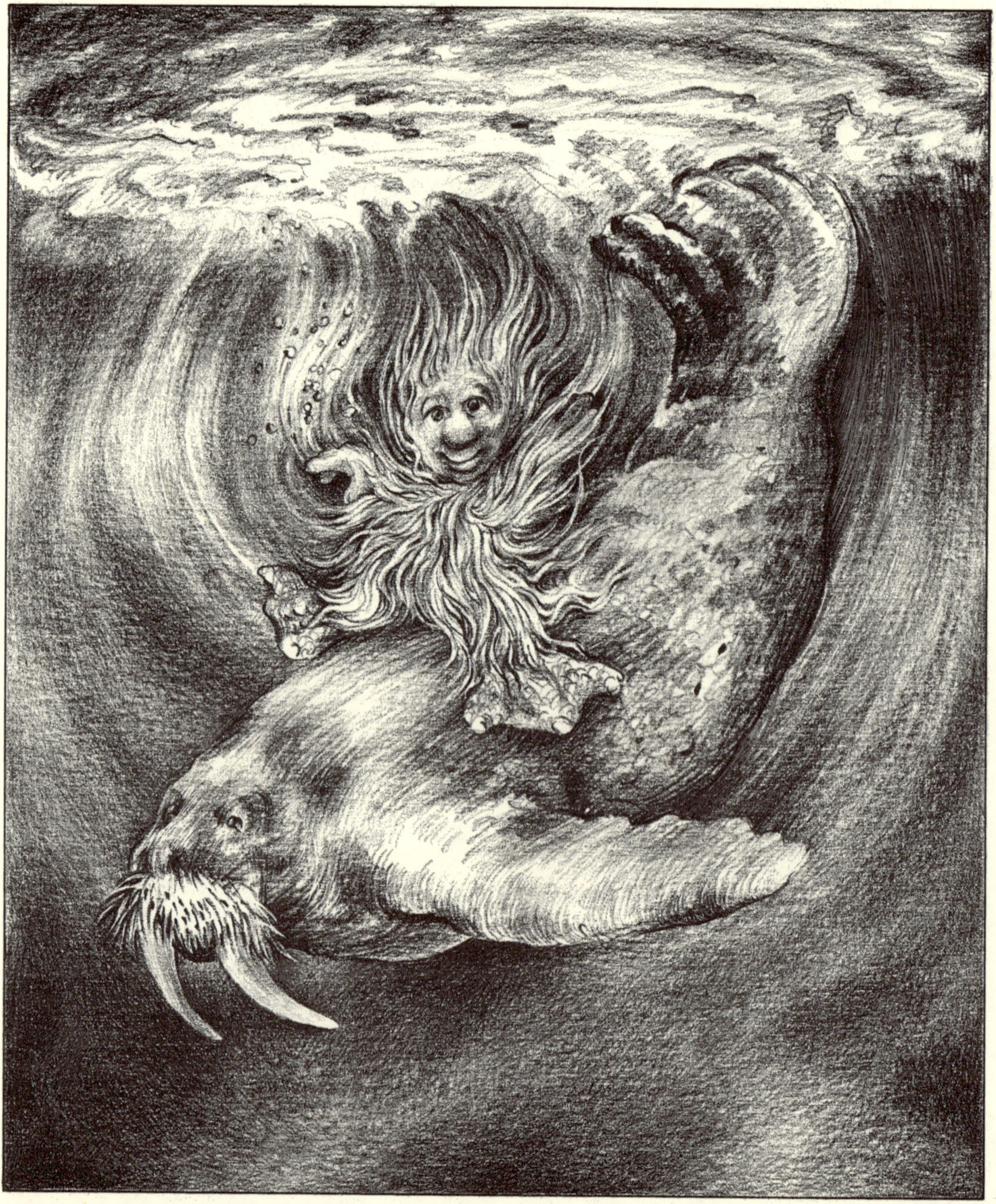

And Nökkungen made the most of it! After all, it's seldom you get to see your leader in such a delightfully ridiculous position! With a bound he was sitting on Dovergubben's stomach, and Vally immediately got the idea. Hooking his tusks gently over the great troll's feet, he began to haul him down the lead.

"The Good Ship Dovergubben!" called Nökkungen, waving.

"Farvel!" called the other trolls.

Soon the Good Ship Dovergubben was moving at a fast clip through the water, while Vally tried to sing the old Norwegian slott.

CRUNCH!! They had reached the end of the lead. What now? Try as he might, Vally could not manage to turn the troll around.

Up on the ice, the others blushed a bit. All this time their leader had not uttered a word. Maybe it was time to get him out!

"I know!" cried Rumpungen. "Sooner or later we must walk around this lead anyway! Let's make our trip shorter and use him as a bridge!"

But the others shook their heads. After all, you have to leave your leader a little dignity! But how to get him out?

"One way sure;" announced Nesa, "we can always make a troll chain." Then she promptly bent over the water so that Dovergubben could get a good hold on her nose. Then Langemann grabbed Nesa's waist. Jotulen grabbed Langemann, Kari grabbed Jotulen, Nökken grabbed Kari, Nökkina grabbed Nökken, Kalvehalen grabbed Nökkina, Rumpungen grabbed Kalvehalen, and Nökkungen scrambled up on the ice to take up the rear. Down in the water, Vally was ready to push.

"Ready?" he called.

"Ready!" they answered and gave a great pull.

With a great SWOOSH Dovergubben was out of the water and sliding across the ice like a sled.

They watched as he stood and shook his coat. Water flew like a rainstorm.

In the meantime, Nökkungen had found the lost eye and now ran to place it in Dovergubben's hand. Quickly he scampered back to his mother. They waited as Dovergubben put the eye in. He stared at them. He glared at them. He looked fiercely from one to the other.

But what was this? Something was flickering around his mouth. It trembled. It quivered. It spread to a smile. In a moment their leader was laughing louder and harder than they had ever heard him laugh before. He roared and gasped and stamped his feet until all the others were laughing too. Down in the water, Vally joined in, until thunder rang in the arctic sky.

Then it thundered below. The trolls looked down. To their horror their stamping had cracked the ice, leaving them stranded on a floating island. Their weight was beginning to sink them down.

"That's just how I saw the humans go!" cried Vally. He had to act fast!

With a tremendous heave, he sank his tusks into their ice floe. Then as he flipped his flippers with all his might, slowly it began to rise. He grunted and groaned, pushing it up, while the trolls paddled furiously toward shore. At last they bumped against the main ice pack.

"*Mange takk*, Vally! *Tusen takk!*" they thanked him as they clambered off.

The time had come to say farewell. Already the night wind was beginning to howl. They would have to find hummock before they could camp.

Suddenly they realized how dark it was. Now all they could see of Vally were his eyes, wide and shining from the open lead. Fog began to close in around them.

"Do you know which way we should go?" asked the trolls.

"No," came Vally's voice. "I wish I did. I don't know much about where the land is. All I know is that I am here...." His voice seemed to trail away in the fog. "And sometimes I even wonder about that...."

The wind whistled. Snow began to whirl. The fog was thicker than ever. Vally's eyes were even harder to see, and they seemed like the only friendly spot in the Arctic. An hour ago they had been strangers to each other. Now they could not manage the words to say goodbye.

Slowly the trolls turned and headed into the dark.

Okpiks and Kiwitaks

Noseward! Ever noseward! Dovergubben had caught a cold from his dunking, so now the others had to depend on their own noses. A sort of sixth sense also helped, for Vally's warmth pulsed behind them like a beacon. Each day it gave them a strong sense of their bearings, and as long as they headed directly away, it kept them from wandering around in circles.

Still, it was dreadfully foggy. They longed to see a speck, a line, a color—*anything* on the horizon!

What they should have been approaching, of course, was northern Greenland, or Perryland as it is called by explorers. But blowing snow often befuddled them, until Dovergubben could only blow his nose and hope his cold wouldn't last much longer.

Then at last they saw it! Black streaks on the horizon! They heaved up their sacks and raced toward the land. How good it would be to stand on solid ground! How good to see plants and animals again! With each hour the streaks grew clearer!

But after a whole day of running, the trolls stopped short.

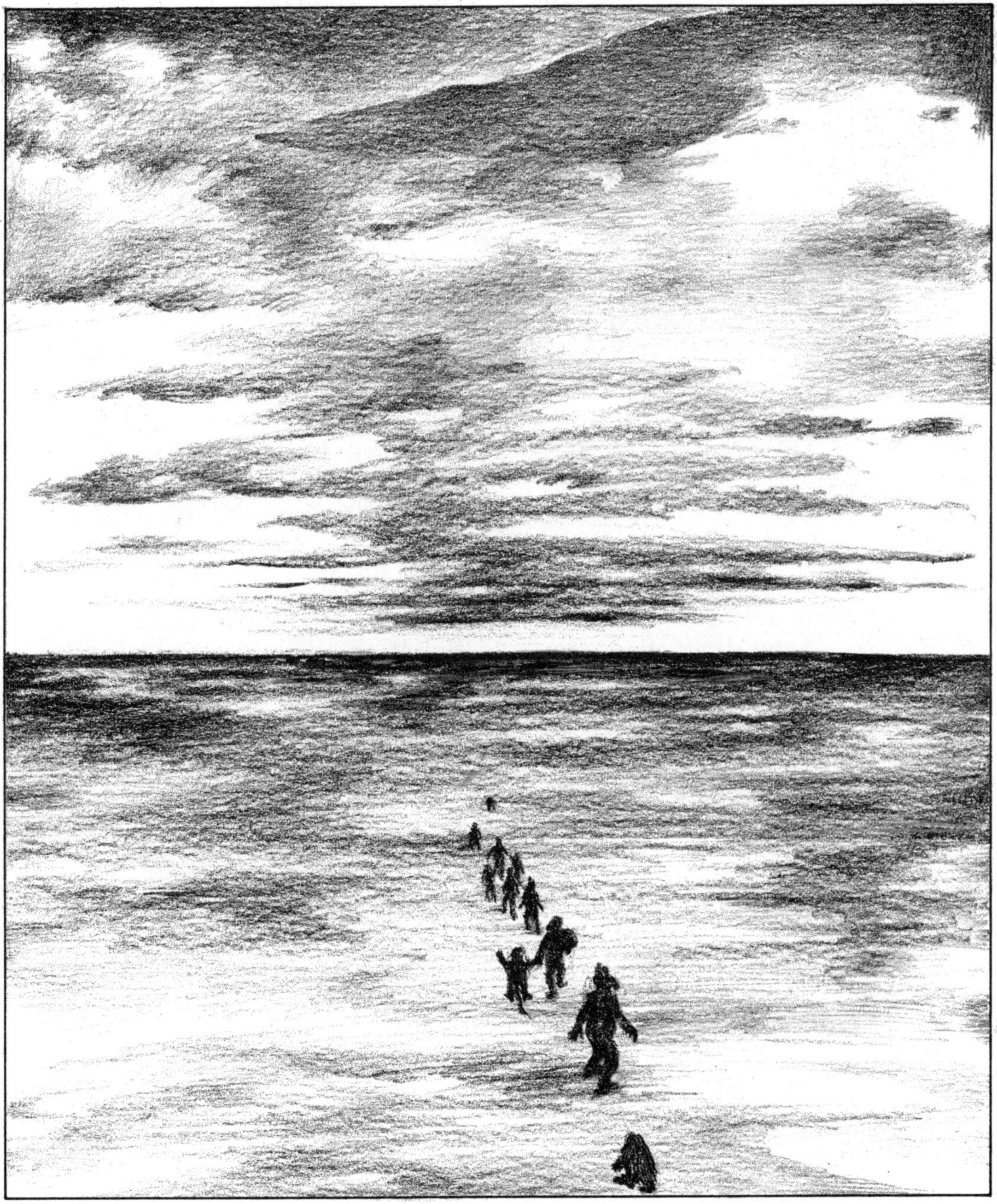

Why, the black streaks were not land at all, but merely more ice! Black ice!

Rumpungen flung himself down. "I thought all ice was white!" he cried bitterly.

The others slumped around him. "Black ice!" they panted. "Black ice!"

Catching his breath, Dovergubben examined the ice closely. "Why, some kind of plant life it is," he gasped. He scratched the surface. "Ja, like tiny leaves gone black with cold!"

He was right, for this was algae, a little plant whose color can range from green to black to pink to yellow. It grows from the equator to the poles, and when it blows on the wind it can make things appear to be what they're not. So if you are ever lost in a wasteland, just remember bright colors may not be what they seem, and don't be fooled by false horizons!

Now the trolls knew how foolish they'd been. Their lungs burned; their legs ached; their spirits had sunk deeper than any ship ever lost beneath the Arctic ice. Now there was nothing to do but make camp behind the strange black hummock. Who could say if they would ever see land again?

They rested for several days, eating, sleeping, and trying to keep warm. Now no one felt the least like singing, so Fosekallen played them old songs from home. Norway seemed a world away, and the New World even farther.

Finally there was nothing to do but head on. They trudged endlessly across the ice. They saw nothing, heard nothing—and nothing saw or heard them.

Then, and who knew how long it had been, they did see something! Sharp black peaks poked up through the Arctic fog. But the trolls vowed not to be tricked as before. They slowed their stride. They tried not to look. But after months of nothing but white, those dark peaks set their eyes all aglitter. How you would have laughed to see them, for even their snail's pace couldn't hide their excitement!

"I do believe it's *land*!" breathed Nesa, when at last they set foot on solid ground. And so it was. The black peaks were *nunataks*, the great mountains of ice that rise from the Greenland ice cap.

Suddenly a squeak rang out! Out of the Arctic fog came the funniest little animals the trolls had ever seen. They bounced and rolled down the slopes, skidding down the glaciers that entered the fjord.

Now the trolls did not know it, but the fuzzy little okpik is the favorite animal of Eskimo children. Sometimes Eskimo parents say that there's no such thing, but of course the children know better. After all, if you see something, it is real! And the trolls certainly saw the okpiks—they were tumbling and sliding all over the place!

Okpiks really aren't very big, only about two feet tall, like Fosekallen. They are fat, white, and furry all over, and the children say they are a cross between bird and mammal, since each one has a sharp little beak. But the very strangest thing about the okpik is that, just like some trolls, each has only one eye. Perhaps this is why they first ran up to Dovergubben. They rolled on their bellies around his feet, squeaking as though he were a long-lost grandfather. Then they saw the troll babies! Squealing with glee, they bounced around them until the troll babies could not help but start bouncing too. Then up the slopes they followed the okpiks, and slid down the glaciers holding the fat fuzzy balls between their feet.

But when they bumped bottom, SQUEAK! the okpiks were off. Away they bounded in a flurry of white, vanishing as suddenly as they had arrived.

"My but this land can keep a troll guessing!" gasped Nesa when the okpiks had disappeared.

And looking around, the trolls saw that it was spring.

You see, along the coast at the edge of the glaciers, there's warmth enough for life to abound. So even though the interior was still quite snowbound, here at the edges spring was creeping in. Red and white heather were already in bloom, and blue saxifrage waved on the wind. All around, the Arctic hares bounded like okpiks, feeding their young ones on new shoots of grass.

The trolls were entranced with each spot of color and ran from one to the other as if they were gems. Then that night around the fire, they sang the song Fosekallen had first sung in Norway. But this time the words had a different ring:

> *Here we sit on the edge of spring,*
> *Where snow dissolves into tips of green,*
> *Green the dream that once called to me,*
> *Green the new land across the sea,*
> *And will it truly Trollhaven be*
> *That we'll find on an autumn wind someday?*
> *That we'll find on an autumn wind?*

The signs of spring filled them with gladness. Gone was the weariness and homesickness of winter. Now, just like the birch whose sap was rising rich and warm, the trolls felt the surge of adventure.

They knew of course that tomorrow they would have to head inland, where winter would surround them once more. But from the wind they also sensed this was an island, and from the wind's fragrance that spring waited on the other side as well.

Off across Perryland they went. Now Rumpungen was hoping they might meet some fellow creatures, and one day on a glacier top he spotted another okpik. "Are there any such things as humans here?" he called.

"Sure," piped the okpik. "Both Greenlanders and Eskimos!" He began to slide down. "But there aren't many real Eskimos left, less than a hundred, last time I counted!"

"But Greenlanders and Eskimos, aren't they one and the same?" shouted Rumpungen.

"Gracious no!" squealed the okpik as he slid. "The Eskimo is a native here and just as yellow as he can be. But the Greenlander is at least half white, and he's the one who's taking over."

He bumped bottom.

Rumpungen ran up to him. "No care have I for what color they are! I just want to know if they'll believe in trolls!"

"Trolls!" squealed the okpik. "Of course not, silly! Humans never believe their eyes! They only see what they're taught to see!" He thought for a moment. "But maybe the Eskimo children will believe in you. One thing for sure, they always see me!"

And with a flurry of white he vanished in the snow.

"Pooh," snuffed Rumpungen. "If *I* were an Eskimo, *I'd* believe in trolls!"

Little did Rumpungen know how soon he'd discover just

what Eskimos *do* believe in! One day, while the other trolls napped, he set out to explore the glaciers alone. He had not gone far when he spotted an animal that stood upright and was brown and furry all over.

"A fellow troll!" laughed Rumpungen, and bounded forward to make friends. *"God dag!"* he called. "I am Rumpungen!"

"And I am Kiwitak!" growled the animal.

Rumpungen stiffened. For though this creature looked somewhat like a troll, he certainly didn't seem to have the good manners of a troll! Still, Rumpungen pressed forward. "Why, what's a kiwitak?" he asked cheerfully.

"A kiwitak," snarled the beast, "is a kiwitak!" And flashing teeth much longer than swords, he took a tremendous leap toward Rumpungen.

Away streaked the baby troll down the ice! The footfalls of Kiwitak thundered behind him! Faster and faster raced the little troll, but his forest feet just weren't made for glaciers. He felt Kiwitak's breath hot on his neck!

Then, KERTHUNK! Rumpungen landed on his belly! Oh, now too late would he know what a kiwitak was! Know him from the inside out!

But nothing happened. He waited. He held his breath. Finally he opened one eye. Above him stood Kiwitak, stark still in his tracks, staring at the huge heap of sleeping trolls. Well, the trolls obviously did not see Kiwitak, but Kiwitak certainly saw the trolls! With a cry of terror he wheeled around and went racing back over the ice!

Only when the beast had completely vanished did Rumpungen dare run to Nesa. Then, as he burbled out his story, an okpik suddenly appeared out of nowhere.

"Oh yes!" squeaked the little fellow. "That was a kiwitak for sure! The children claim he is cruel and vicious and raids their Eskimo camps by night!" And, WHISK! the okpik was gone again.

Well, you can imagine how the incident upset the other troll babies, and for days they would not venture out on the glaciers.

Yet spring was on the wind! Each day drew them nearer the scent, until at last there they were, camped in the west coast's heather.

In the distance stretched another sea of ice, but this one at least had no mist or fog. Behind them Kiwitak was but a memory. Before them, the New World beckoned.

Bowheads and Iceboats

Now if you had wakened with the trolls the next morning, you would have been a bit worried too. Overnight the spring wind had loosened the ice, and open leads were everywhere. In one just ahead spouted a group of bowhead whales.

"Ahoy!" called the lead whale when he saw them. "What brings you to these northern waters?"

"Twelve trolls are we!" called Dovergubben. "To America we travel!"

"And might we make your passage easier?" bellowed the whale.

Visions of Kiwitak rose in the trolls' memories.

"What have you in mind?" called Dovergubben.

Swiftly the whales crossed to where the trolls were standing. "A dozen trolls and a dozen whales!" spouted the leader. "Hop aboard! We'll cruise you across!"

Well, he certainly seemed friendly enough. And who ever turned down a chance for a lift? So the trolls clambered onto the slippery backs, and away they sailed.

Now if you ever straddle a bowhead whale, be sure to place your fingers in his ears, and this way you will find that you can steer him. Press the right and he will turn right; press the left and he'll turn to the left. This is exactly what the trolls now did—all but little Rumpungen, that is! Away he went, pressing right when he wanted to go left, pressing the left and going vice versa. This confused the whale and made him dive, which of course the other trolls had to try too. Soon trolls and whales were all laughing and plunging. But Rumpungen kept forgetting to hold his breath. Down he would swoop deep under the surface, and then shoot up spouting more water than his whale. Finally, though, he got the hang of it.

How the whales frolicked! In and out of the leads they dived, rolling and reeling around in circles. In fact, the trolls began to wonder if they ever intended to make the crossing at all! But after a while the whales seemed to tire and began cruising steadily west.

How lovely to lie on a whale and go sailing! Overhead the sky whisped from grey to white, and the trolls spotted animals among the clouds. Kiwitaks, okpiks, foxes and seals drifted lazily overhead. Soon the trolls were fast asleep.

"Wake up, you landlubbers! You're on Ellesmere Island!" spouted the whales.

Indeed they were! Still half dreaming, the trolls slid down the whales' backs. "*Farvel!*" they called. "*Og mange takk!*"

A dozen sprays spouted off in the night.

The trolls looked around. Suddenly they were wide awake. A shrill wind was slicing through their fur, bitter cold like blades of ice! Just like the warning they'd heard long ago...*of a place where the wind...where the wind*, it whistled, *cuts like a knife...like a knife to your bone!*

Ah, surely this was that place and that wind! But there was nothing in sight to shield off the blasts. In a second they were massed together, arms, legs and bodies intertwined.

Suddenly they heard the sound of hoofs! Looking around, they saw a furry shape, galloping swiftly away through the dark. Maybe it would lead them to warmth! Still clinging to each other, the trolls followed. From behind, the animal looked something like a large calf, but this was surely no dairy variety!

When it stopped behind a bluff, there were dozens more like it, but bigger! Massive brown animals they were, with horns that curved down and flared to either side of their chins. All heads turned, and the horn tips glistened.

The trolls could not move. Who could say whether it was from cold or fear, but their muscles had frozen stiff as ice. Now all they could do was stare and shiver as the beasts began closing in around them. They squeezed their eyes shut. Oh, now they would feel just how sharp those horns were!

But then, how strange! They felt only warmth, only the softest, thickest fur in the world. The animals were rubbing up against them, gently rocking to and fro.

"Birds of a feather should flock together," lowed the calf with a little nudge. Why, the animals were trying to keep the trolls warm!

"Ahhh, m-mange t-takk!" stuttered Fosekallen. "Without you w-we would have f-frozen sure!"

"Take some fur," mooed a soft-eyed cow. "After all, it's shedding season."

So the trolls sat down with the great animals bunched around them, and Grandmother Kjerringa began shaping hats from their wool.

"Surely you've n-not seen trolls before," said Fosekallen, once his shivering stopped. "Are you always so k-kind to your f-fellow creatures?"

"Not to the other two-legged ones," brayed the bull. "But you looked different—and deathly cold."

Then the trolls explained who they were and that they were traveling to a place called the New World.

"But what are *you*?" they asked the strange animals.

"Musk oxen," mooed the cow, "ancestor of all sheep and oxen."

"And have you ever been to America?" asked Fosekallen.

"Not I," answered the cow. "But during the ice age our ancestors roamed far to the south. Then when the ice moved north, so did they. I suppose that's how we ended up on Ellesmere."

A startled look crossed Fosekallen's face. "Maybe you'll not believe this," he began, "but I swear I once saw a picture of you painted on a cave wall back home!"

"One of our ancestors, no doubt!" chuckled the bull. "So maybe we were once fellow countrymen!" Then he explained that their present home, Ellesmere, is the first link in a long string of islands which lead to a land called Canada. "And Canada," he said, "is where the New World begins!"

Suddenly the trolls were full of questions. They wanted to know more of the lands ahead, so they decided to camp among the musk oxen that night.

"But only if you wear my hats!" insisted Grandmother Kjerringa, and she firmly pulled one over Dovergubben's head.

"Trolls don't wear hats!" Dovergubben protested.

But then he overheard the musk oxen telling of all the other expeditioners who had passed this way. "And they all wore hats," the bull was saying. "Though none so warm as musk oxen fur."

So Dovergubben relented. Through the long night the musk oxen told them stories of lands they'd heard the explorers describe. "And they say the cold lingers far to the south—so keep those hats!" warned a cow.

Well, the trolls had weathered cold before, but even Dovergubben had to admit that with his head covered, his whole body felt much warmer.

"Of course, during the day you won't need them," the cow continued. "For it's growing warmer and the ice will soon be breaking up."

"That's right! If you really mean to go island hopping, you'd better be on your way, and soon!" brayed the bull.

So all at once it was time to go. Once more the trolls stood wordless and silent, wondering how to say goodbye.

"Watch out for sump holes!" the calf finally called out.

So with this tender and curious farewell, the trolls set out once more. Now they would travel the winding straits from Devon to Baffin to Somerset to Victoria.

Signs of spring were everywhere! High overhead soared the Arctic terns, glad to be home after their winter in the Antarctic. By the time the trolls arrived at Devon, they found auks and puffins making nests. Fulmars were flying by the thousands, and this time you can be sure Jotulen kept his distance. Then off they set for Baffin Island.

Now all had been going along quite well, when one day

the ice gave a tremendous lurch. Instantly the ocean opened up all around them, and each found himself on a separate ice floe! Anyone else would have panicked, of course—but never trolls! Being Norwegian, they are natural navigators, and they realized that if each of them could stay afloat, the current itself would bring them back together.

And so it did. By evening they had all banked safely on Baffin Island. Here the song of the ptarmigan rang back and forth among the hills. Spotting a few, the troll babies raced them and chased them, just to hear the rush of their wings on the wind. And had the trolls been human explorers, they surely would have feasted on "northern fried chicken" that night. Instead, they ate berries, and when they had finished they lay back to feast their ears on the ptarmigan's rich song.

The next day they pushed off on their ice floes once more. Now Fosekallen began to sing of Canada! In fact, one morning he was so lost in his fiddling, he didn't even notice when his floe suddenly changed direction.

You see, the trolls were sailing toward Amundsen's Gulf, where the current travels in two directions—one whisking you into the gulf, the other just as quickly whooshing you out. Well, you can guess which current Fosekallen got into! Away he sailed, fiddling his heart out, with no idea he was headed back to Norway!

Suddenly the others realized what was happening. They shouted and called, but Fosekallen was too far away. Seal heads started popping up from the leads, looking to see what the cries were all about. In a flash, fjord seals, harp seals, ring seals and Greenland seals all went rushing to Fosekallen's rescue. It took every one of them pushing together to get the

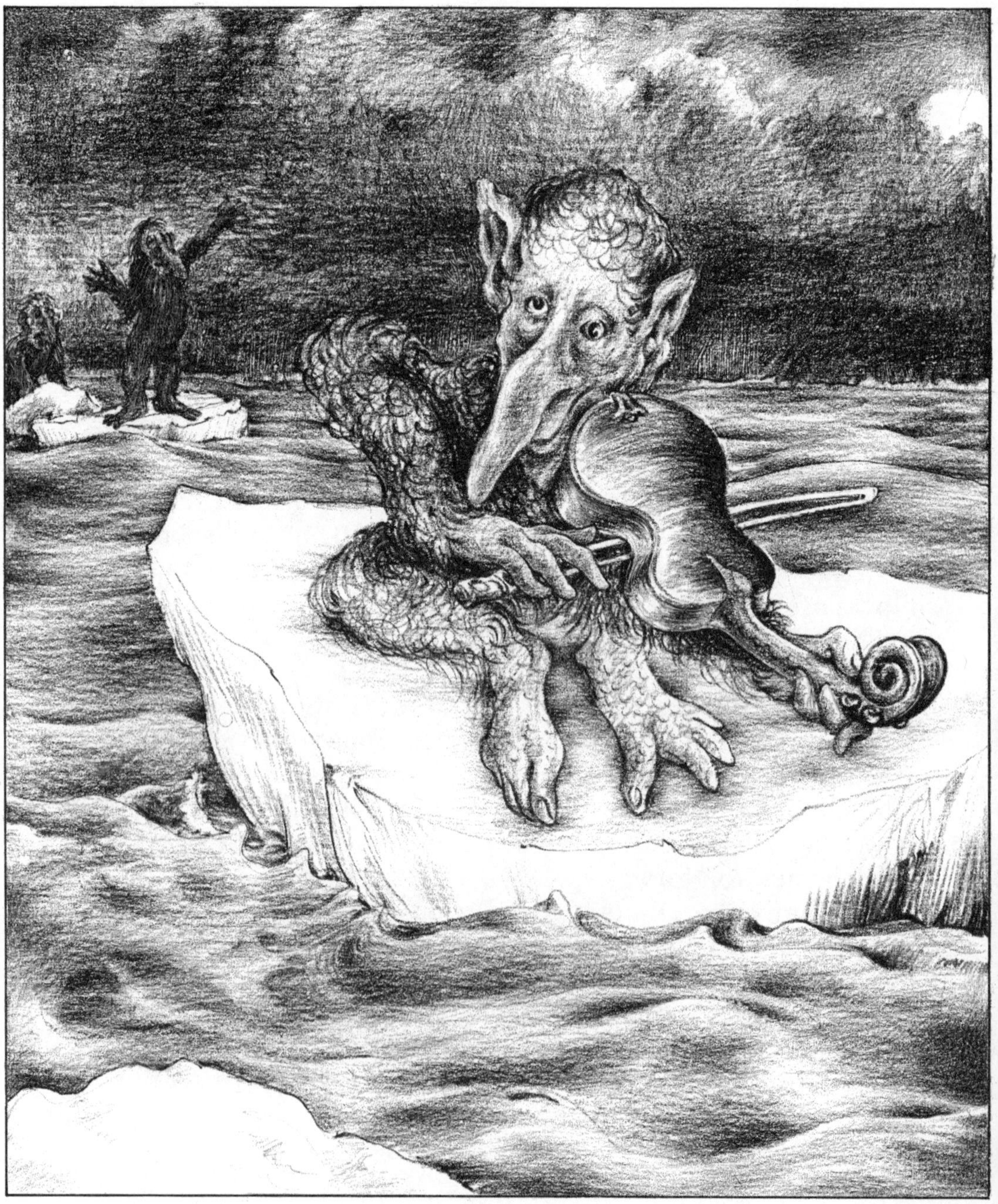

startled fiddler back on course.

Poor Fosekallen. He was stuttering much too hard to thank them. Instead he drew his bow and began to play. When he finally reached the others, he was surrounded by seals!

Nökkungen was delighted, for among the seals were several small babies who were just learning to swim. Like young trolls or even humans, the pups blundered clumsily into their parents, making all sorts of ridiculous sounds.

"It's about time I had somebody to swim with!" cried Nökkungen. "If only your parents would guide us to Canada!"

"Well . . . would the little troll fiddle as we went?" asked an adult seal.

"Of course!" laughed Fosekallen. "All the way!"

So it was a merry party that headed for Amundsen's Gulf. The seals with their babies, the trolls on their ice floes—all went singing along with the wind and the waves.

That night the trolls camped on Somerset Island, the next night on Victoria, and after that on smaller islands. Finally one day a field of water opened before them.

"Amundsen's Gulf!" yipped the seals.

The trolls remembered Storegubben's stories. Why, this must be named for a fellow explorer! And they looked at the sunny blue water in delight. All except Grandmother Kjerringa! She was staring, horrified, at the seals. "But Storegubben said it was the *South* Pole Amundsen discovered!" she cried. "You've made a mistake! You've taken us too far!"

"Of course not! This is Canada," the seals barked. "Your Amundsen probably made some discoveries here, too! This is the Northwest Territory, the mainland of the New World!"

The New World!

With many thanks, they bid the seals goodbye and, a little dazed, stepped onto solid land.

Here flowers bloomed! The sun shone bright! In fact, a little too bright for trolls! Scurrying to the shadows, they realized it must be May. They counted on their fingers: *en - to - tre - fire - fem - seks*. . . . It was May sixteenth! Exactly a year had gone by since the night they had first dreamed of this journey!

They decided to camp a bit inland from the gulf, and as on all past eves of Norwegian Independence Day, they built a fire and sat in a ring. For the very first time in their lives, they were not on Troll Tinderne for the celebration.

The thought sank in them like a stone. Storegubben and all the trolls of Norway—they'd be gathering now around the fire! Troll-Elgen and all the animals—they'd be singing, and soon the dancing would begin! At the thought of dancing, the trolls' heads sank even lower. Why dance for Norway here? Why dance for anything, with their friends so far away?

As if he'd heard the clunk of their spirits, Dovergubben raised his head and spoke. "And have we not friends now all across the Arctic?" he asked. "And in places we never had hopes of even one?"

Immediately they thought of Vally; they thought of the musk oxen, hares and seals, of the okpiks, foxes and bowhead whales. They thought of the times they'd danced on the ice. And all at once, they *did* feel like dancing! Up they leapt! Ja, it was truly May sixteenth! They danced all the old dances and sang all the old songs, feasted and frolicked and told old tales. Today they had reached the New World!

But would Storegubben know? Perhaps they should sing a message to the wind and hope it would carry over the sea. The words came to them easily enough, and as they sat weaving them into a tune, a warm wind began to blow. Softly, the trolls sang it their message:

> *O listen, you trolls*
> *On Troll Tinderne's crest,*
> *Do you hear how the wind moves the pines?*
> *The boughs of the birch trees*
> *All sway with our song,*
> *And Sperillen's ripples keep time.*
> *The heather is singing!*
> *The bluebells are ringing!*
> *We've reached the New World today!*
> *And now as the wind blows*
> *O'er Tinderne's last snows,*
> *May it melt all your worries away!*

Then they lay back and gazed at the stars until it seemed even Nanook bore them no ill.

At dawn came a whoosh of wings. Blue and grey geese were taking to the sky.

"Where do you go?" called Fosekallen.

"To our nesting grounds in the north," they answered.

"And where have you come from?"

"From a land to the south, a land called America!"

In the faint morning light the trolls looked around and smiled. Ja, they were getting closer!

Nesa's Nose

Now the trolls had to be careful! Each day the sun spread his rays a little wider, turning inlets to open water, snowfields to slush, and trolls to.... Not quite! They were too careful for *that*! Now they traveled only by moonlight.

Full moons were best, especially for bounding across the tundra! Only if you have walked across a mattress with sponges on your feet will you appreciate what it is like. The trolls loved it, especially Kari. With a squoosh and a slosh she skipped along, for some reason growing prettier by the day.

Only Nesa didn't enjoy it. You see, her nose had gotten quite bent out of shape from carrying Nökkungen and from pulling Dovergubben out of the lead. Now it bumped along in everyone's way. "Watch it," she grumbled at Kari one night. "What a humiliating way for a nose to travel!" she grumbled a little louder.

And the more she grumbled, the more her nose sagged, until one day she tripped over it and fell flat on her face. When she tried to get up, she found her nose was stuck in a deep boggy hollow. Poor Nesa! Try as she might, she could not get free! And to make it worse, the other trolls had started to chuckle. Now they realized what the musk ox calf had meant! So this was a sump hole!

There was nothing to do but form another troll chain. Langemann grabbed Nesa's waist, and all the others linked on behind. *"En - to - tre!"* They heaved and hauled and tugged and groaned. "EN - TO - TRE!" Suddenly they all went tumbling backward, and with a FWUMPTH! the nose was free at last.

Well, as you can imagine, it was in worse shape then ever. It took four logs to splint it, one hundred and fifty yards of tundra grass to bind it, and Nesa was in a fouler humor than ever. Like a black cloud she lumbered off across the bog, supporting her heavy splints on Langemann's shoulder.

"You're going too fast," Nesa would grumble, and when he slowed down, "You're such a slowpoke!"

After three nights, Langemann could take no more of it. "One more grump, and you carry your own nose," he warned. "Ah, when will we ever take a rest?"

Just then Fosekallen came winging by. "Wh-what a pair!" he tittered at the two. "Now not only is N-Nesa's nose out of joint, but L-Langemann's got a big chip on his shoulder!" And, still tittering, he flew ahead to find a resting place.

In no time he was back. "There's a b-beautiful lake not much farther on!" he sang. "With trout at least twice as big as m-me!"

TROUT! Off bounded the lake trolls, their webbed feet sloshing joyously across the tundra. Even Nesa's spirits soared! "A tasty trout!" she cried happily. "Just what my nose needs!"

The trolls all broke into a run. Their noses were pointing

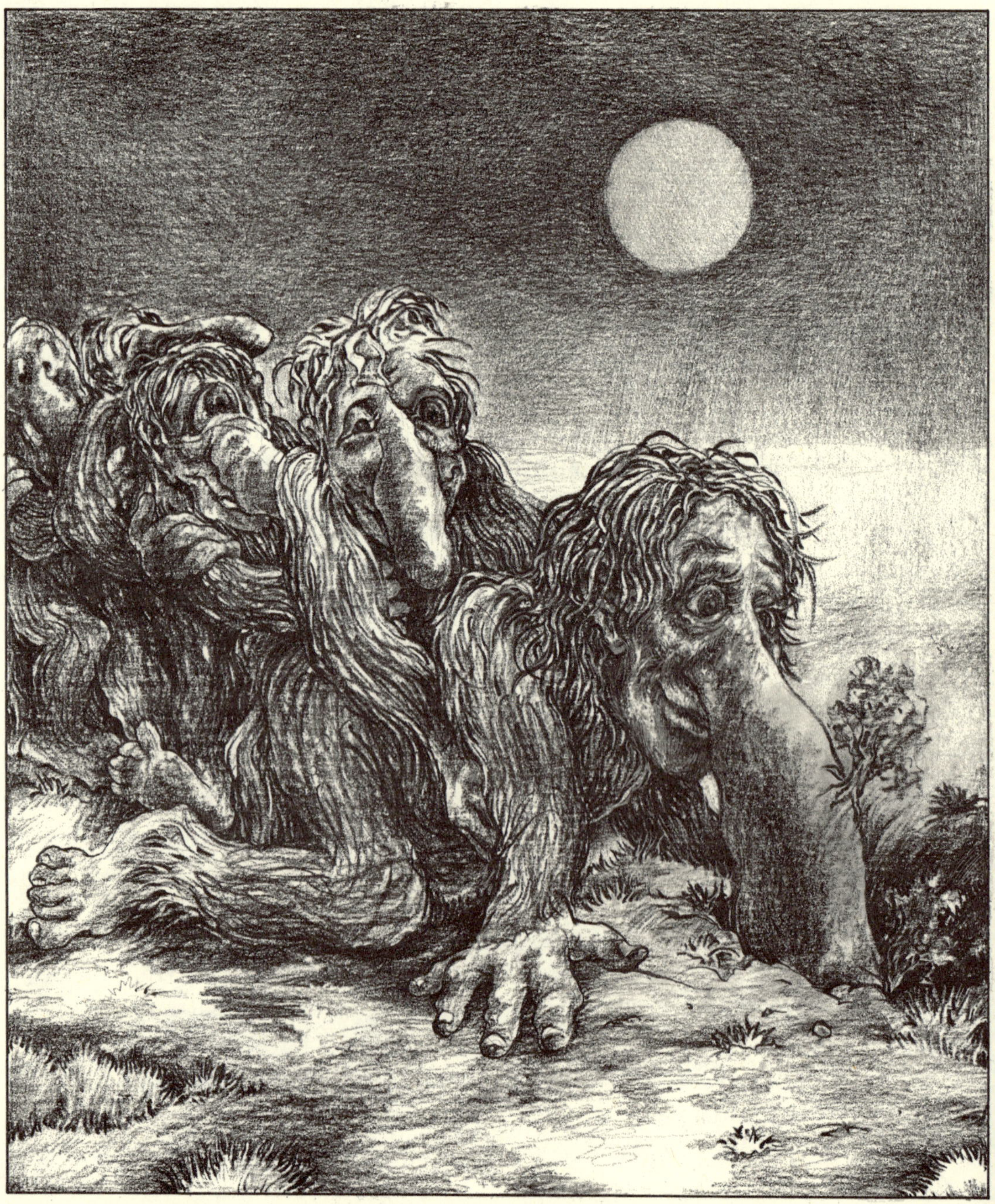

them straight at Great Bear Lake, the largest lake in the Northwest Territory, and the home of enormous trout and grayling. They arrived just at dawn, the perfect time for fishing.

But alas, they were too late! Nökken and Nökkina had already made friends with the fish. Typical lake trolls that they were, Nökkina had enlisted the grayling to give Nökkungen a life-saving lesson, while Nökken was teaching the trout escape and evasion! Now who had the heart to go fishing?

"How can a nose heal without fishmeal?" Nesa protested as the others went off to gather mushrooms. "Mushrooms, indeed!" Nesa sniffed.

Still, mushrooms seemed to help, and after two days (though Nesa denied it) her nose was feeling much stronger. Now the others volunteered to help Langemann shoulder the load, and once again they set off across the tundra.

Three nights later, with sagging shoulders, they came upon another lake. "Bother," grumbled Nesa when she saw the lake trolls already splashing happily with the fish. "Let's just cross and be done with it!"

Their hopes of a fishmeal feast dashed again, the others quickly agreed.

However, "just crossing" presented more of a problem than you might think. For this was the Great Slave, a lake at least three hundred and sixty miles long and heaven only knows how deep. Even at the Narrows it is too deep for trolls.

Anxiously they gazed across the water. Nökken and Nökkina could swim it, of course, and Fosekallen could fly. But what of the others?

"Kari and I would sink like stones!" groaned Jotulen. "There's no way for us but to walk around."

"And I suppose we forest trolls could float across like logs," said Dovergubben with a glimmer of a smile.

"And hope my nose doesn't drown me in the process!" grumbled Nesa.

"Or capsize under the weight of the troll babies," added Langemann.

Nesa's eyebrows shot straight up. "You think I'm going to carry babes on this nose? And it in its pitiful condition?"

Wearily the trolls glanced at one another. Who would bear the nose this time? And who would take charge of the little ones? But before anyone could rush to volunteer, two animals came splashing across the water. One looked something like a reindeer, and the other could almost have been Troll-Elgen himself!

"Troll-Elgen! Troll-Elgen!" called the troll babies, rushing up to him.

The animal balked. "Elgen!" he snorted. "I'm no elk! Don't you know a moose when you see one?"

"Moose!" sneered Nesa. "What a silly name. You're an elk as surely as our great Troll-Elgen!" And she told him of his Norwegian cousin who opens all the ceremonies on Lake Sperillen.

"He sure sounds like a moose to me," sniffed the animal.

Just then a third animal appeared, with a narrower nose and high, graceful antlers.

The animal who'd always thought he was a moose sighed enviously. "There's your elk," he said.

Nesa groaned. "No, that's a wapiti! Just ask him and see!"

80

"Of course I'm a wapiti!" said the newcomer, without waiting to be asked. "At least that's what the Indians call me. It was those foreign settlers long ago who made a mistake and called me 'elgen'."

"So you see? He's a wapiti and you're an elk, and there's no such thing as a moose!" declared Nesa. "Unless that reindeer fellow calls himself a moose!"

"Reindeer fellow!" snorted the third animal. "I beg your pardon! I'm a caribou!"

"*Caribou?*" Nesa's eyes began to glimmer. "Carry what?" she asked slyly.

"US!" shrieked the troll babies. And before Nesa could say "my nose!" they had leapt to the three animals' backs and were galloping headlong into the lake.

Well, that took care of the troll baby question, but Nesa was glowering down her nose like thunder. "Somebody's got to help carry *this!*" she said.

"I suppose we three can float beneath it like a raft," sighed Langemann, glancing at the other forest trolls.

"That's settled, then," Nesa snapped.

All the rest were glad to be taking separate routes. After all, they had been in each others' company all the way from Norway, and even trolls need time to themselves now and then.

So Fosekallen took to the sky, the lake trolls splashed into the water, and Kari skipped off to meet Jotulen. Now a mountain troll's skipping isn't exactly delicate, and Kari's made the whole lake wobble and slosh.

"Leave it to Kari to drown us in a tidal wave!" growled Nesa.

"Leave it to Nesa to find harm in a pretty mountain troll!" chided Grandmother Kjerringa.

But Nesa kept right on grumbling. The forest trolls set themselves afloat beneath her nose, grateful to find that the water muffled all her grouching and snorting.

Then what a circus! Forward steamed Nesa, spouting and fuming, while the troll babies splashed ahead on the backs of their new-found friends. They had discovered that by pressing antlers instead of ears, they could steer these animals as they had the bowhead whales. Squealing and giggling, they plunged in circles around the forest troll raft. Wapiti, elk and caribou loved it, glad, of course, to be carrying troll babies instead of that nose!

"Let's race!" called the elk when they had all tired of circles. "I'll bet I can reach the other side first!"

The troll babies crowed with delight. "*Hypp! Hypp!*" they cried, kicking their heels, and the animals raced through the water neck and neck.

Kalvehalen took the lead. Then, to get even further ahead, she suddenly leapt to the top of her caribou's antlers. Startled, he flung back his head, and poor Kalvehalen flew off, screeching in surprise!

Just at that moment, who should come floating by? PLUNK! Kalvehalen landed on her mother's nose. In one great lunge, Langemann had his daughter by the tail. "High time it is you learned to hang onto something!" he shouted. With that, he knotted Kalvehalen's tail around the tail of Nökkungen's elk.

"*Hypp! Hypp!*" he shouted, giving the elk a slap.

Off across the Narrows went the elk, dragging the troll

baby sputtering behind. Of course the elk was losing the race by now anyway, so he slowed down so that Kalvehalen would not be hurt.

"*Mange takk* for going so slow," she thanked him when they finally reached shore. Her caribou had won the race. "Without your weight, how I flew!" he said, gratefully nudging Kalvehalen.

"If it hadn't been for her father, *I* would have won," sulked the elk. "He certainly wasn't in a very nice mood."

Kalvehalen blushed. "Ja, all the big trolls have been acting so—ever since my mother got her nose caught in a bog."

"Bogs!! That's all anyone ever sees in the tundra," snorted the elk. "Why, look how it's bursting with flowers and lichen. How can anyone be grouchy when the tundra's in bloom?"

"How can you be grouchy when the tundra's in bloom?" asked Kalvehalen when her parents finally floated in to shore.

"In bloom?" cried Nesa. "The tundra, you say?"

Langemann looked at his wife in surprise.

"Why did no one tell me?" she asked, craning her neck, trying to see over her splints.

And only then did they realize that all this time, Nesa hadn't been able to see past the end of her nose.

Now she pleaded with Langemann to take off the splints. Langemann frowned. What if her nose should sag again? What if this time it broke for good? Still, her eyes were so filled with excitement that he slowly began to unwind the tundra grass. Gently he lifted off the splints.

He almost dropped them! For there on Nesa's mountain ash trees were hundreds of tiny white blossoms! Why, she hadn't bloomed like this for two hundred years! Tenderly, Langemann put his arm around his wife and led her to the water so she could see her reflection.

Whether it was her blossoms, the moonlight, or the loon's song across the lake—something had changed by the time the others arrived.

"You know," said Nesa that night around the fire, "the spring is very much improving our health! Why, look at Kari! She's more in bloom than my nose. And it makes me want to sing!"

That was all Fosekallen needed. With a flourish he drew his bow, and as he fiddled, Nesa sang a new verse:

>Now we travel a starlit way,
>Where flowers dance on the tundra gay!
>Over the lake comes the cry of the loon.
>Over our heads shines a smiling moon.
>O Norway, do you still hear our tune,
>That we sing on a springtime wind, faraway?
>That we sing on a springtime wind?

There was no doubting it. Nesa's nose had healed!

The Lore of the Southlands

The elk, or moose as he calls himself in the New World, had made his point. What a shame to see only bogs in the tundra, or be so intent on some little dot on the horizon that you miss all the flowers in the foreground. Suddenly everything around the Great Slave seemed to burst into color—the tundra, the granite, the mosses and lichen! And so the trolls couldn't resist staying just a bit longer.

You see, trolls have a peculiar habit, one a human might laughingly call "feasting the senses." Still, silly as it might look, this feast of the senses is just the sort of nourishment trolls can't live without. Now they rolled in the grasses, sang back to each bird call, and gulped the wind's fragrance until you'd have sworn they were drunk! No wonder they reeled a little as they set out three days later!

Now they wound their way ever southward among small lakes where whooping cranes were nesting. Was that the plains they sniffed on the wind? Sure enough, after many nights, an open range spread out before them.

But how strange! Ahead of them stood—could it be a musk ox? But musk oxen are polar animals, and besides, this fellow's horns curled to the front, not the sides.

"A buffalo!" shouted Dovergubben. "Storegubben told me of these!"

Forward bounded the trolls, calling the animal by name, ready to embrace him like his kinfolk on Ellesmere.

The shaggy beast slowly raised his great head.

"Buffalo!" he bellowed indignantly. "Call me Bison!"

Well, having learned that the animals in this new land don't necessarily know their own names, the trolls didn't let that stop them.

But the animal lowered his horns. "They do not pass who call me 'buffalo.' *Bison* is the name of the king of the prairie! Buffalo turn water wheels on the other side of the world!"

"And h-how do you know of the world's other side?" stuttered Fosekallen.

"I listen," replied the animal. "I listen to the other two-legged creatures who pass. I listen and I learn."

"You mean humans?" asked Dovergubben. "Would you tell us of them? For we are strangers here and have much to learn about this land."

"Wait," grunted the bison. "I must ask my elder."

When he had turned, the trolls glanced at each other. Certainly this was a proud beast! And so intent were they on watching him go that they did not notice when the troll babies slipped away.

The trolls watched as the bison became a tiny speck on the horizon, then disappeared. "His elder must be far away indeed," said Grandmother Kjerringa. "It may be a long time before he returns."

"We will wait," said Dovergubben. So wait they did, until

even Dovergubben began to doubt that the animal was ever coming back. Suddenly the ground began to shiver under their feet. Then it shook, harder and harder, and the trolls heard a low rumble that grew louder and louder. And like clouds thundering across the plain they came—the whole herd!

They stopped in a whirl of dust. In front was an ancient bearded one. "Why do you come?" he asked.

"Why, we..."

But before Dovergubben could answer, they were all surrounded by squeals and grunts. Here came the troll babies astride three baby bison, with dozens more romping about them! Round and round the range they galloped. They bucked and bounded and bumped together until they all went tumbling head over tail over rump! Over and over each other they rolled, until neither the bison nor the trolls could tell one of their furry babies from another.

The old one let out a gruff chuckle. He squinted at the trolls. "The little ones trust each other," he said. "Perhaps it's the young who should teach the old."

"Surely you did not take us for humans," said Dovergubben.

"We're wary of anything that walks on two legs," sighed the ancient one. "But you are different. I can see that. Of the Tribe of Sasquatch, I suppose."

"No, of the Trolldom of Storegubben!" Dovergubben corrected. And then he explained where they had come from. "So much we do not know of this land," he added, "and mostly we want to know all about its humans."

"That would take all spring," grunted the bison.

"B-but we haven't t-time . . ." Fosekallen began.

"Then at least stay the night," the old one replied, "for I think you all could use a rest."

"Ja," said Kari, "we should rest, I think." All the trolls turned and grinned at her. "If Kari wishes," Dovergubben said.

Graciously a bison offered Kari a ride as the others trooped over to a grove of trees.

"And why should he carry *you?*" grumped Jotulen when they were all seated in the grass.

The old one chuckled into his beard. "Even a bison father knows why the cow's hair suddenly grows so warm and thick!"

At that all the trolls had to chuckle too. Hadn't Jotulen noticed? For just like all mothers-to-be, Kari had been growing prettier by the day. Now her hair hung thick and lustrous to protect the little one before its birth. And just like the flowers on Nesa's nose, Kari seemed to be in bloom. She blushed, and Jotulen stared and stammered until his teeth clattered like a rockslide.

"Wh-when?" was all he could say.

"In the autumn," Kari beamed. "When we've reached America!"

"America?" groaned the bison. "Hmmmph! I wish you luck!"

"Why?" asked Dovergubben. "Is something wrong?"

"Wrong? No. Changed? Yes! Even here it's different than before they came," said the bison.

"Who?"

"They who put us here. Don't you know?" demanded the

bison. "This is the Canadian Bison Refuge, the one corner we're allowed to roam, the home we're supposed to be grateful for!"

"But why . . . ?" Dovergubben began.

"And they've done the same with the Indian," the bison continued. "Though for him it's called a reservation."

"Is an Indian anything like a troll?" Nökkungen asked eagerly.

"Not at all!" the bison chuckled. "The Indian is human. Still, Indian and bison shared the land in nature's way, and though he hunted us, he always thanked us for the hunt."

The bison sighed. "It was the others, the ones with guns, who nearly wiped us from the earth. Some of our ancestors escaped here to the north, but of the hunts to the south, nothing more was ever heard."

"Well, I'm afraid it's to the south, to the land of those 'others,' that we go," said Dovergubben.

"Why? Do you seek something there?" asked the bison.

So Dovergubben told him of the search for Trollhaven and repeated the story that Storegubben had told. "Way back eleven hundred years," said Dovergubben, "the wind spoke to our Master of a land to the west. Far over the ice and tundra and plains, so it said, lies a land as fair as our Norway. The wind spoke of a mountain as lovely as Tinderne and a lake as blue as the blue of Sperillen."

Suddenly the bison's eyes gleamed. "Yes," he said. "A land of bright water. A land of high towering mountains. I once heard an old Indian speak of it. I don't recall what the word means, but I think he called it *Ee-da-how!*"

"Ee-da-how!" murmured all the trolls. Was the land of the

Indians the land they sought? Had it once been there? Would it still be there?

"Perhaps if I were younger, I would seek it myself," sighed the old one.

Camped among the bison, the trolls learned much about humans, or at least of the red-skinned humans of long ago. Some of their deeds were as terrible as the Vikings' and some as noble as the land itself. But America? The bison were not sure. Perhaps at Ee-da-how the Indian was still king.

"Ee-da-how!" How the word rang through their dreams! Land of bright water! Land of towering mountains! Suddenly the plains seemed incredibly dull.

"Won't a few of you come with us?" asked Dovergubben the next night. "For if we find it, surely others could then follow."

But the bison only shook their heads. "The hunts," they grunted, "might not be over."

"Farvel, then!" called the trolls, and with the vision of Ee-da-how to spur them they hurried eagerly on their way.

On they went. The nights grew warm. They crossed another lake, the Lesser Slave. On and on the flatness stretched, as the summer moon shone cool upon them. And they say, the children of Alberta, that shadows crossed their windows that summer, shadows of trees where no trees grow.

Finally, after what seemed forever, Jotulen spotted bumps on the horizon. *"Fjell!"* he roared. "Just what Kari needs! Mountain air in her lungs to make the troll baby grow!"

And so the trolls now turned westward—or rather, noseward! They walked through moonlight; they walked through starlight; and sometimes they used the stars as guides—

especially when they lost sight of the mountains. The plains seemed to go on and on.

"Those mountains, maybe they were a trick like the black ice," sighed Kari, scanning the horizon one night.

"Ja, b-but could the stars and our noses b-both be wrong?" asked Fosekallen.

Suddenly a growling sound came from on high.

"Crazy trolls! You're too impatient!" growled a voice.

The trolls looked up. Why, there was Nanook, right where Nesa had thrown him, staring grouchily down at them.

"Can you see if we head the right way?" called Nesa.

"If I could, I wouldn't tell the likes of you!" growled the bear.

"B-but just now you said we were too impatient. Wh-what did you mean?" called Fosekallen.

"And so you are!" growled Nanook. "But that's all I'm going to tell you!" Then he chuckled and waited to see what they would do.

Well, what *could* they do but go on, and hope his gruff words had been encouragement in disguise?

Two nights later they reached the mountains.

"Tusen takk, Nanook!" they called to the sky.

Ah, here it smelled just like home. The scent of pine rose from the forest floor, and tiny flowers pushed up through the rock. Up they went, tracing a river that bounced and cascaded down from the highlands. Here the mountains are called the Kootenais, and though the trolls didn't know their name, they wondered if the Indians had once made them their home.

Then one night, Dovergubben stopped short in his tracks.

Beside the sandy bank was a huge footprint. One by one they placed their feet next to it. It matched Jotulen's exactly. Could it be that other trolls roamed this land? Canadian trolls? Indian trolls?

Well, being typical trolls themselves, they had to find out! Along the river's edge they followed the prints. Soon they began to find dark hair hanging from the branches, hair which looked almost like their own!

Of course, the trolls weren't the least afraid. But well they might have been, had they known that this is the land of Sasquatch! Said to be part human and part animal, Sasquatch roams the mountains of the West, and legend has it that he is not the sort of creature you'd want to bump into in the dark of night.

But knowing none of this, the trolls tracked him eagerly. How lucky it would be to find a fellow troll! Maybe he would even join the expedition!

They'd gone but a little way when they spotted fresh wet tracks in the sand. Their eyes wandered up the river to the left, through the trees, to the bluff to the . . . . There he was!

He was not very big, only about ten feet tall, and he sat slumped on a rock with his head in his hands. In fact, he looked for all the world like a scolded troll baby.

"Shsh," whispered Dovergubben. "Let the little ones go first. That way he won't be frightened by our size."

Softly, Nökkungen, Rumpungen and Kalvehalen approached. Then so gently did they place their hands on the creature's shoulders that he was neither startled nor angered. Instead, he turned sad eyes to the trolls. "You are newcomers to this land," he said, "for you don't yell and run from me."

"Do others run from you?" asked Rumpungen, suddenly recalling Kiwitak.

"Only humans. And now they run *at* me!" sighed Sasquatch. "They call me Big Foot. They chase me with their dogs and cameras! They hound me to prove I might exist!" He shook his head. "It's awful being a legend."

"Why, in Norway it's fun!" laughed Kalvehalen. "All the people believe in trolls! You should see how they grin and chuckle when Rumpungen and I pop out at them!"

But Sasquatch only shook his head.

Gently, the other trolls gathered around him. They opened their food bags, built a fire, and invited the loner to eat with them. That night, for the first time in his life, Sasquatch ate with fellow creatures.

"You shouldn't have come here," he said when they had finished. "Word will get around and they'll hound you like me."

"But did the Indians hound you?" Rumpungen wanted to know. "For it is to an Indian land we go."

"No, but they kept their distance all right," Sasquatch grunted. "Indians are human too."

"But have you heard of a land they called Ee-da-how?" asked Jotulen.

Sasquatch sat up straight. "I *have* heard of such a place," he said. "And if I knew where it was, that's just where I'd . . ."

"Then come with us!" cried Dovergubben. "For it is there we go to find our Trollhaven!"

"Ah, ja!" urged Kari. "No good is it to be alone! With us you will always have a family."

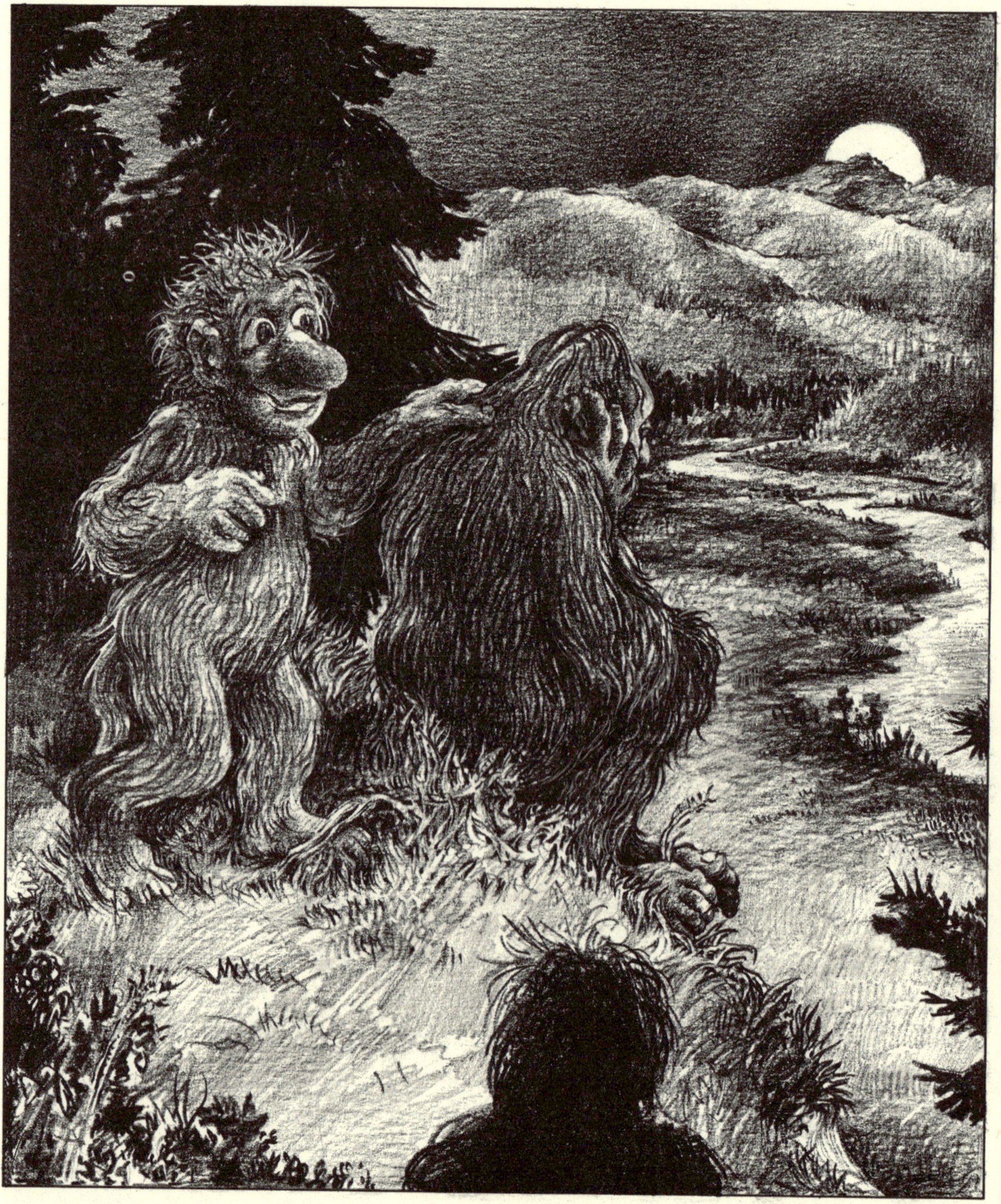

But at Kari's last word, Sasquatch slumped. His head sank down between his shoulders. "I'm not of your kind," he muttered. "Everyone in nature has creatures like himself. But look at *me*—a misfit, a freak!"

"But nature, she does not work that way!" insisted Kari. "Somewhere you must have a mother or brothers or . . ."

Slowly Sasquatch raised his head. "Why do you think I roam these mountains," he asked, "searching year after year, age after age?" Suddenly he looked very weary. "Only yesterday a bison said he'd seen something like me down in Oregon. That's where I was headed when you came along."

"But maybe you'll never find them!" Kari said.

"Still, I must seek!" Sasquatch stood up and gazed around the ring of trolls. "If I fail, I guess I was just meant to live alone," he grunted.

Then with a gruff nod of farewell, he lumbered off into the darkness.

Around their campfire, the trolls sat very still. Were they the only creatures who still danced in the fields, who rolled in the flowers and got drunk on the wind? They thought of the hunted. They thought of the hounded.

Ah, but they were trolls! Mostly they thought of Ee-da-how!

The Eagle's Way

Something about Sasquatch kept troubling the trolls, perhaps just the sight of his trail through the dust. Now they followed it over a ridge in hopes they might spot him in the valley below. But it was no use. He was lost down there somewhere among the hills.

The view, however, made them quiver. Such a fair green land they had never seen, and it seemed to stretch on forever. "Could this be America?" they asked each other.

One look at Dovergubben's nose gave the answer. Never had it pointed so unwaveringly ahead.

"I shall fly high and scout the way!" called Fosekallen. And with a flurry of feathers he soared above them as an ouzel.

No words could describe what the troll-bird saw then. But imagine yourself flying over moonlit mountains, looking down on rivers like ribbons below. Imagine high crests still glazed with winter, and dark lakes still surrounded with snow. To Fosekallen those lakes seemed like sleeping goslings, nestled secretly in the woods.

"Ah," he sighed. "This could well be Norway!"

Suddenly, out of nowhere came a piercing shriek! Wings beat hard above his head! A pair of claws snatched at his feathers! Looking up, he saw an enormous bird!

"Sp-spare me!" cried Fosekallen. "A t-troll am I!"

The bird stopped in mid-air. "A *what?*" he demanded.

But Fosekallen could only point to his friends down below.

"Holy Moses!" squawked the bird. "What in tarnation are they?"

"T-trolls!" stuttered Fosekallen. "And so am I. Just let me land and I'll prove it!"

Well, the bird seemed curious enough to see if this was true, and he dove straight for a treetop above the trolls.

With a bump, Fosekallen made it to the ground; then he instantly changed himself into a troll again.

"Why, I'll be bamboozled!" squawked the bird.

Startled, the rest of the trolls looked up. What they saw was a great brown bird, and the crown of his head was snowy white.

"Hee, hee! It looks like a bald spot!" giggled Rumpungen.

"Okay, laugh!" rasped the bird a bit testily. "But us eagles are the pride of the country! Symbol of justice and all that jazz!" He cocked his head. "And what box of Cracker Jacks did you guys pop out of?"

"Boxakrakerjax?" echoed Dovergubben, bewildered. "I know of no such country as that. Trolls are we, out of Norway, and we search for the land called America."

That set the eagle wheezing with laughter. "But this whole blessed continent is America! I think what you mean is the U.S. of A!"

"The yewessuvay?" blurted Dovergubben. "What is that?"

"Land of the free! Home of the brave! And the skies are not cloudy all day!" sang the bird.

"That must be it!" said Dovergubben. "Is it such a fine place as they say?"

"The best!" squawked the eagle.

"And might you show us the way?" Dovergubben asked.

"To the U.S. of A? Sure thing!" squawked the eagle. "The border guard is only a few miles away!"

Border guard?

And before they knew it, the trolls had learned a whole string of new words: *customs, contraband, alien, immigration, passport* . . .

"Only you don't need a passport just to come in from Canada," the eagle assured them.

But they'd still have to cross the border! Would the humans at the guard station be able to see them? And if they could, would they understand Norwegian?

"Ja, and suppose they should send us straight back to Norway," said Grandmother Kjerringa. "Then all our long journey will have been in vain!"

"Don't worry," the eagle assured them. "What the border guards don't know won't hurt them. You don't have to cross at the guard station. I'll lead you in a roundabout way."

Still, the trolls had no desire to be sneaky, and it took the eagle a long time to convince them that, like the migrating geese, they too were free travelers.

Early the next evening, he guided them over the border. Then what a celebration there was! They feasted on delicacies from all over the Arctic, and just as the last light faded from the sky, the eagle cocked his head.

There was a tremendous boom!

"Just as I suspected!" he winked. "The Americans are celebrating your arrival!"

Suddenly the air was filled with colored lights. Red streaks and shooting stars burst in glorious patterns. Each time, there was another loud boom.

The trolls could not believe it! How had the Americans known they were here? But when they asked him, the eagle only smiled and winked knowingly. "What difference does it make? Enjoy it while it lasts!" he said.

The trolls didn't need any further excuse! Soon their dancing thundered through the night—a night that will long be remembered at the border. In fact, if you ever visit the northernmost towns, just ask and the people will tell you of a mysterious Fourth of July, when their houses shook until long after midnight.

Now the trolls felt better about sneaking over the border, especially since the Americans had welcomed them so warmly. And later, as they sat around the fire, they asked the eagle to stay on as their guide.

"Well, that all depends on where you're headed," he said. "And if I know where the place might be!"

And so the trolls told of the land the wind spoke of, the land of Storegubben's long-ago dream. "Even the bison and Sasquatch have heard of it," said Dovergubben," and call it by the name of Ee-da-how!"

"Ee-da-how!" screeched the eagle. "You crazy trolls! That's exactly where you are!" And he laughed at them until the tears rolled down his beak.

"But how were we to know?" murmured Kari.

The eagle peered round at their baffled faces. "Aw, maybe I shouldn'ta laughed so soon," he apologized. "You guys don't know anything about this place, do you? Well, I'll tell you a story I once heard about its name. *Ee-da-how* was what the Indians said when they saw the first morning light. Sorta like saying *wow* and *hello* at the same time. It was their greeting for the new day and also their word for *light on the mountain*. Folks say that in one particular place, the Indians saw that light—well, almost like magic. It was a place known only to them, you see, where for a second the sun burst like a gem on the summit."

"And do you know where that place might be?" breathed Dovergubben.

The eagle cocked his head and squinted. "I have a hunch," he answered. "That is, if you want to take a chance."

"A troll will always take a chance!" laughed Dovergubben.

The eagle said that it wasn't far, and the following evening they were on their way. High above them soared their friend, a tiny dot against the sun's last rays. Then down he would swoop to make sure they were following, and at each landmark he called out a name:

"Lake Pend Oreille! Lake Coeur d'Alene! Now, trolls, we're following the Saint Joe River!"

Finally they stopped in the Bitterroot Mountains. Never had they gone so far in one night! Now at dawn they wearily lay down in the shadows, and the eagle perched above them to guard their sleep.

"But you must sleep too!" the trolls called to their friend.

"Okay! But I'm gonna keep one eye open," he answered. "Never know when that sneaky sun might try turnin' one of you guys to a pile of rocks!"

The trolls fell into a deep sleep and didn't open their eyes until sunset. When they awoke, the sky had turned to a sea of gold, and their eagle's dark shadow sailed upon it like a ship.

"C'mon, let's get going!" he called, flapping his wings.

"We're coming," they answered, and they were on their way again.

All through the night they hiked rolling highlands. Toward dawn they arrived in the Clearwater Mountains.

"Sun's comin' up! Better make camp!" called the eagle.

But now the trolls were too excited to sleep, and they begged the eagle to guide them on through the day.

"Well, just be careful! This area is rocky enough," he warned, "without you trolls contributing to the problem!"

The eagle was right. It was the most rugged country they had traveled so far. Trying to keep to the shadows of the peaks, they began climbing down cliffs and rocky basins. It was about noon when they realized they had lost sight of their eagle. Far below they could see two rivers merging. If only their friend were here to name them! They wondered if they should go down.

Well, as the eagle could have told them, one of the rivers was the Salmon, also known as "the river of no return." The other was its southern fork, and along both a few old mountain men still roam.

Sure enough, suddenly they saw a man! The first human of their entire trip! He had a long white beard, clothes made

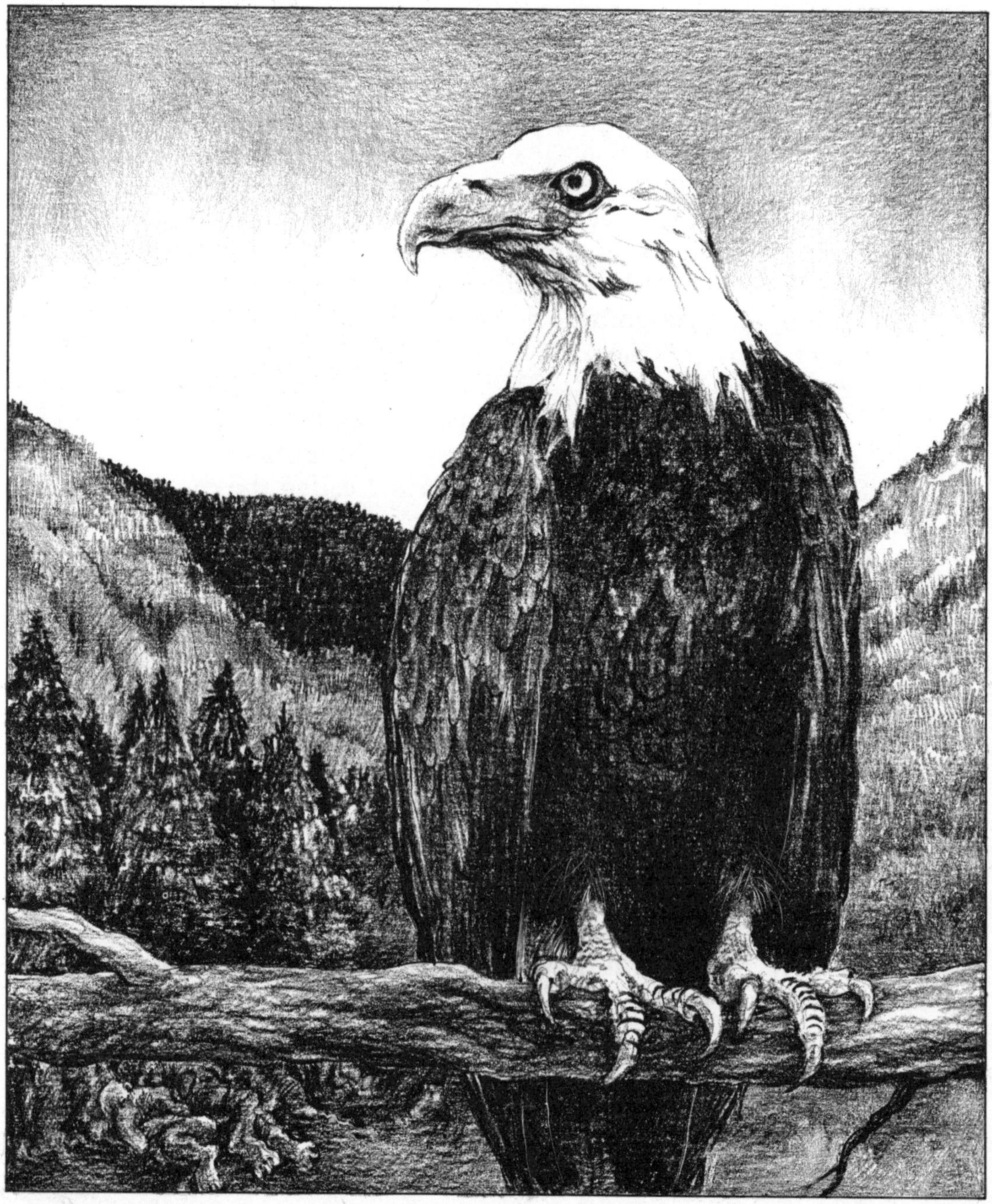

of hide, and a bearskin helmet.

The trolls crept closer. "He looks like a billy goat to me" whispered Rumpungen.

"Not a billy goat, silly! That's buckskin he's wearing!" giggled Kalvehalen.

"I say billy goat!"

"I say buckskin!"

"No, billy goat!"

"Buckskin!"

At last the children compromised and named the fellow "Buckskin Billy."

"Buckskin Billy, can you see us?" they whispered.

The man cocked his head and squinted toward the trees.

"Hush!" warned their parents. For even though the man had friendly eyes, they weren't sure what he might do. Quietly he went back to whittling his stick.

The trolls moved still closer, stopping just above the man. He was humming softly to himself, scratching in the dirt with his stick. Gradually they began to feel at ease, as though he would not even start if they should walk right up to him. Still, they waited until he had moved on.

"Do you think he saw us?" Nökkungen asked when they reached the spot where the man had been sitting.

"Ah, no," said Nökkina.

But barely had she spoken when something made her halt. Scrawled in the dirt was a long word: SKOOKUMCHUCK!

Skookumchuck?

Something rustled in the trees.

"Run!" yelled Dovergubben.

Off they plunged into the woods, running faster and faster, afraid to look back.

"Slow down!" a voice suddenly screeched from high above them.

It was their eagle. "What's the hustle!" he demanded.

Dovergubben blushed. "A human we saw! And with a stick he wrote us a warning!"

"What warning?" asked the eagle.

With trembling hands, Dovergubben picked up a stick and traced SKOOKUMCHUCK.

Then how their friend laughed! He screeched and squawked and bounced around until he almost fell off his branch.

"That means 'welcome'," he managed to wheeze at last. "It's another old Indian word!"

The trolls glanced sheepishly at one another. They knew so little about this land that their eagle was forever laughing at them. And something else they didn't know was that from his perch their eagle could see down the river to where Buckskin Billy stood laughing too!

All afternoon they trekked along, and the eagle chuckled down at them from time to time. In fact, the trolls began to wonder if this whole trek was just a joke to their friend.

That night around the fire, they began to ask questions. "This place you take us to—have you been there?" asked Nökkina.

"Why sure!" said the bird, blinking at them and looking a little hurt.

"It's just that you haven't told us much," added Nökken. "What is it like there? Is there a lake, and fish?"

"Sure!"

"And how about humans?" asked Nökkungen.

But the eagle didn't seem to want to talk anymore. "Maybe I just like to keep a surprise," he mumbled.

Yet from the way he clawed the ground and kept glancing away, the trolls guessed something was bothering him.

The next day he was even more touchy. He lagged behind as they hiked along and frowned whenever they tried to cheer him up.

"Such peaks as these always make me sing!" called Kari from the shadow of a mountain.

"Don't!" squawked the eagle. "What good are songs? All they do is make you sad!"

With each mile he seemed to go more slowly; but finally, toward evening, they came to a ridge.

"The Secesh River!" the eagle called out, laughing a little wistfully. "And the metropolis of Burgdorf!"

Well, the trolls didn't see what was so funny, and with noses twitching they peered over the ridge at the town.

"It's nothing," called the eagle. "C'mon, it's time to camp."

But the trolls kept staring over the cliff. Here were soft grey houses whittled smooth by the wind, and a few small corrals with cows and chickens.

Then they caught their breath, for at the end of the meadow stood a triangular tent, like the ones the bison had said the Indians once lived in. Could this be an Indian village? A flap opened and two shaggy-haired humans stepped out. The trolls sighed. No Indians were these, for they were as fair-skinned as Norwegians. Still, their eyes looked as friendly as Buckskin Bill's.

"Come on!" sighed the eagle. "I'm awfully tired."

So after a few more glances the trolls turned and followed.

"Those humans seemed to have such quiet ways," said Kari when they had sat down around their fire. "Are you sure that was not our place?"

"Nope," said the eagle. "Yours is a little further on."

"Is there a town near the place we're heading?" Kari asked.

"Yup," he replied.

"Well, from the eyes of the humans we've seen today, I think surely Americans will see us trolls!" Grandmother Kjerringa smiled.

The eagle cleared his throat as if to say something, but then he looked troubled and turned away. You see, Burgdorf is almost a ghost town, and the few people who live there are not really typical Americans at all. The eagle said nothing of this, but cocked his head as the trolls talked eagerly of their new homeland.

"By this time tomorrow, who knows?" said Kari. "Maybe we'll have already named it Trollhaven!"

"Trollhaven," the others sighed. "Ah, will it be the land of Storegubben's dream?"

The eagle just sat blinking in silence. Silently he listened to the song the trolls now sang:

High we walk the eagle's way,
Where bluebells ring and waterfalls play.
Over the hills in the dark of night,
We're off to a ridge of crystal light!
O Norway, do you still think we might
Find the dream that we dreamed back home, long ago?
Find the dream that we dreamed back home?

For a moment the eagle hugged himself with his wings. Then he flapped them and suddenly took to the air. "You're on your own!" he called down to them.

The trolls' mouths dropped open in surprise.

"Don't worry," the bird called, hovering for a moment. "Just head straight south and you'll find it for sure. Big lake—you can't miss it!"

"B-but aren't you coming too?" stuttered Fosekallen.

"I'd like to, sure!" the eagle called. "You know, travelin' with you guys, this land looks almost new!"

But he was already high overhead.

"See, when I met you, I was following some other eagles who were headed for a place called the Great Slave Lake," he squawked. He circled up and around again. "Gotta get back on the track!" he called. "Take care—and keep an eye on the sun!"

Then higher he soared, growing smaller and smaller.

"*Mange takk!*" called the trolls as the tiny dot disappeared.

Still they were puzzled by the eagle's flight. Why did he leave them? Was he playing a joke? But his parting look had been as warm as Vally's. Ah, maybe he just wanted the discovery to be theirs alone!

The next morning nothing could have stopped them. Eagerly they set forth on their own. Over rocks, ridges, and creeks they scrambled, avoiding the sun, and always following Dovergubben's nose.

The forests were emerald, the mountains blue-grey. Yes, surely this land was made for trolls. Now at each crest they paused and held their breath. Would this be the place?

Toward noon, Nökkungen suddenly gave a squeal. "There it is!" he cried. "The lake Storegubben spoke of!"

Sure enough, tucked in the mountainside was a little lake. SPLOOSH! Nökkungen was in with a bound!

"Not yet," laughed Dovergubben, dragging him out. "Our land lies to the south and west."

The others sighed. They too had thought this might be it.

"I know!" insisted Dovergubben. "Look at my nose! See how it points ever ahead!"

"It wouldn't if you'd ever look down," grumbled the soggy troll baby. "Your nose only knows what it wants to know."

Dovergubben snorted and continued along the ridge. What could they do but shrug and follow? Better not to get your leader's nose out of joint. Heaven knows where you might end up then!

Now, every time they wanted a better view, they had to head up another slope, and another, and another. Their legs ached. If only their eagle still flew above them!

Suddenly at the top of yet another crest, all their noses jerked and pointed downhill!

They gasped. For there, straight down the slopes of their noses, spread like a banner in the valley below, was a lake! A long, crystal-blue lake! It was ringed with mountains, fringed with pines, and along one shoreline nestled a town.

"Ahhh..." breathed Dovergubben. "This is it!"

Ee-da-how

But as Dovergubben drew his breath, he began to sneeze. His lips turned blue, his nose turned red, and he must have sneezed at least sixteen times!

Frantically, the other trolls pounded his back. But wait! There was another noise! Above Dovergubben's sneezing came a dreadful drone. It was as if their eyes had opened anew. Now they saw motorboats all over the lake. Shops and businesses crowded the shore, and from the town's center came the glare of chrome. All the trolls were sneezing now!

You see, even if the air is fragrant with pine, a troll nose can always pick up the faint underscents. Burning garbage, sewage, oil—no smell escapes the nose of a troll.

Nor can words express the feeling that then swept over them. Nine months and thousands of miles ago, they had dared dream of this place. Was this their answer? Was this what they had sought?

For once Dovergubben had no words at all. For once his eye only stared at the ground. Then, like a great tree giving way at the roots, he sank slowly to the forest floor. The others did the same. They wanted neither to think nor feel. For in this, trolls are very much like humans: whenever things get too great for them to bear, they simply lie down and try to sleep. Perhaps it is the illusion that dreams take you away. Ah, but even troll dreams cannot keep out the truth. Now as they slept on top of Brundage Mountain, nightmares began to darken the lands of their dreams. Forests withered, skies blurred with smoke, and through them a bedraggled eagle winged his way.

Yet as the trolls slept, quite a different thing was happening. The sky blushed pink, then deepened to orange. It blazed to scarlet, then softened to mauve. Slowly the night came with its purples and blues, until like a star-studded bowl it arched over the lake.

Only then did the trolls awaken. How changed it all was! Now the only sound was the sweep of the wind blowing the smells away.

"It must be late! Look how bright the North Star!" whispered Dovergubben.

The troll babies gazed up at the night sky. Could it be that the stars which had guided them across thousands of miles were these very same stars now shining over the lake? But then they began to giggle. They wriggled and snickered and pointed to the sky until at last Langemann asked what was going on.

"He followed us here! He followed us here!" they laughed.

"Who?"

But the troll babies could only giggle and point overhead.

"Ah," chuckled Langemann. "So he did!"

You see, whenever you sit on Brundage Mountain, the Big Dipper hangs right over the lake. So all it takes is a bit of squinting before Nanook appears, glowing white as a star.

"When will you trolls learn to follow your noses?" he now grumbled down at them. "I can see where you're headed and you're not there yet."

The trolls' eyebrows shot up. "Why, where should we go?" they called up to the bear.

But Nanook wasn't about to tell. "You threw me up here! You find you own way!" he growled.

Still the trolls could not help but thank him. But where to go? He had said that they must follow their noses. And which way did their noses point?

"DOWN!" they all said at once.

So down they went. They skirted the sleeping town, crossed a low ridge, and began following a dirt road. But where were they going? Would it be far? How would they know when they finally got there?

They looked up. Nanook winked. The trolls glanced around them. It was very still. Uncertainly they turned from the road and were immediately faced with a wall of brush. From somewhere close came the cry of a loon.

Slowly they parted the brush. They blinked. There, waiting as if it expected them, was a little lake. Here were no shops, no odors, no noise—only the soft lap of waves on the shore. In the moonlight a mountain rose against the sky.

"Could this be it?" Jotulen whispered.

"Where the morning light shines at the edge of the mountain," the others murmured.

"Then for morning we must wait," said Dovergubben.

The trolls sat down. Kalvehalen snuggled close to her mother. "Is this it? Is this Trollhaven?" she whispered.

Nesa smiled and cuddled her child against her breast. "I know not but what Storegubben told us," she answered. "A voice will come to us on the wind, like a voice we once heard in our dreams long ago."

Just then there was a rustle in the forest. Slowly a pale light stenciled the mountain's edge. It glimmered a moment, then burst in the center, blazing like a diamond.

"Ee-da-how!" breathed the trolls.

They had seen the first sign.

Dawn moved across the sky. Like faint music, she spread her first hues until slowly they swelled in a crescendo of color.

The trolls lay back and watched. But how heavy their eyelids! One by one, without even realizing it, they all fell asleep.

Now another music played around their ears, the music of bird song, of wind in the pines, of water rippling down over the rocks. The wind seemed to whisper, *"God morgen, troll, god morgen!"*

The trolls shifted in their sleep, dreaming of voices they had known long ago.

"God morgen," whispered the wind, and then a little louder, "God morgen, troll!"

The trolls sat up with a start. What was that voice?

"God morgen!" the wind rustled in a bush.

Dovergubben squinted his eye. "Name the three rivers which meet in a lake," he breathed.

"Vågå, Lesja and Lom," answered the bush.

"And what is the day when trolls gather near that lake?"

"The sixteenth of May," answered the bush.

"Ah, and by what name do they call that lake?"

"Why, Sperillen, to be sure!" came the voice. And still speaking in the trolls' native language, it went right on. "The lake is easy enough to find, if you take the road sixty kilometers from Oslo. Then making your way through the birch and pine forests, you'll see a mountain known as . . ."

"Troll Tinderne!" cried Grandmother Kjerringa. "Dovergubben, we have found our home!"

"Indeed you have, Kjerringa!" said the bush with a shake.

And to the trolls' amazement, out stepped a man! His hair was white as dandelion fluff, and his bright eyes mirrored the lake and trees. Best of all (and they could tell by his stubborn jaw), this was a fellow Norwegian!

"Velkommen!" said Dovergubben.

"No, no—it is I who come to welcome you," grinned the white-haired man. "Since a year ago May, I've dreamed of nothing but trolls. And now look! Here you are, just where I dreamed!"

Had it been possible, they would have all hugged him at once. But being only five feet nine, the man presented a bit of a problem. Finally he used Nesa's nose as an elevator, and the hugging and nose-rubbing was properly accomplished.

Then they sat down to breakfast. There was much to ask this fellow countryman. Mostly they wanted to know if they could stay here. Could they really make this land their home?

"Well, like all water, Little Lake belongs to no one," said the man. "But this land we are on belongs to a doctor. He lives in a house past the trees over there."

"Ja, but will he mind if trolls live here?" asked Kjerringa.

"How can he when he can't even see you?" chuckled the

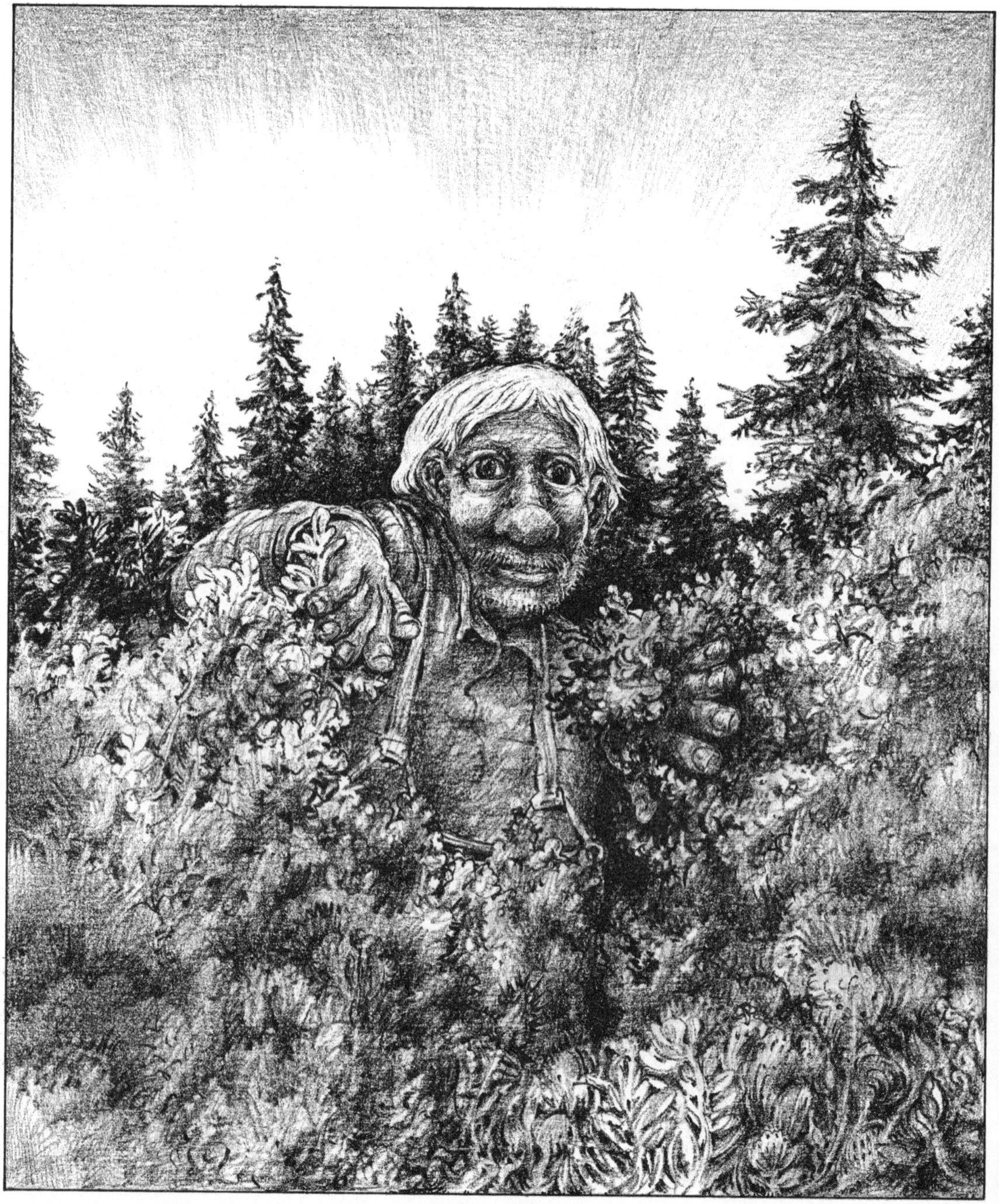

man. "Ja, for you it's a good thing I'm here. Otherwise, how could you exist?"

"You mean people won't believe in us here?" asked Rumpungen wistfully.

Gently the man reached out and ruffled Rumpungen's hair. "Ah, they have a hard enough time believing *I'm* for real! You can hardly blame them for doubting trolls. Still," he added, "I have a few friends I'm teaching. Mostly they're people who live in town—Carolyn, Carl, and a mother named Ann, who has two children, Holly and John. There's the Nelson family who live nearby, and a tall girl and her husband who want to believe. Then there's Björn the Swede, who shouldn't have to be taught about trolls."

"Is that all?" sighed Rumpungen.

"Well, let's see. There are some to the south—Chris and Steve and Little Claire; an artist; and a couple named Marty and Suzanne. Then to the north there's a lady named Sister. She is very conservative, but she likes the idea," said the man. "But the worst one of all is our friend the doctor. I tell him, but he refuses to believe."

"Hmph!" snorted Rumpungen. "And what would become of humans, I wonder, if trolls decided not to believe in *them*!"

"That, Rumpungen, is a very good question," replied their new friend, standing up. "But for now, it's time to find you some homes."

Being a Norwegian he knew, of course, that a troll's home is not a house. First he led the lake trolls down to the water. "Two children drowned there once," he said, pointing to a deep spot. "So if you want to protect children as you do in Norway, that would be your wisest choice."

Next they strolled deep into the woods, where Dovergubben and Kjerringa chose a spot. Here beds of fallen branches would keep in the warmth, while the trees' thick trunks would ward off the wind. Likewise, their friend showed Langemann and Nesa a clearing in the trees, this one a little farther up the river near the old sheep bridge.

"And look!" said the man, pointing downstream. There a little ouzel was flying over a waterfall. As the bird swooped to the shoreline, Fosekallen could tell it was a female by the way she gently dipped her tail.

"I th-think I'll l-live there," Fosekallen stammered.

Now only Jotulen and Kari remained. "And there's no doubt where you belong," said the man. He glanced up to the east. "It's called Jughandle, though why I don't know."

"But you do know trolls, and well!" smiled Kari. "For you've shown us the very things each of us needs to feel at home."

"All but one!" winked the white-haired man. "And I know just the spot!"

Curious, they followed him down to a big meadow.

"I named it Troll Meadow—for the Council of Trolls," he grinned. "Even Storegubben himself couldn't ask for a finer!"

The trolls gasped. "You know Storegubben?"

But just then an osprey called across the lake.

"Coming!" called the man. He winked at the trolls. "He always gets impatient when it's time to go fishing."

And with that he disappeared back into the bushes.

Velkommen

The trolls blinked as the white-haired man departed. Who could say just where he had come from or how he had known that they would be here?

Maybe someday it would all be explained. For now, the important thing was that they were here, here in the spot Storegubben had surely intended. Yet, what roamed these mountains and swam this lake? Would the animals take kindly to a trolldom?

"Please can we go exploring?" Kalvehalen and Rumpungen begged their mother.

"Only if you keep to the shadows," Nesa warned. "For I have no wish to mother a rock pile."

Of course Nökkungen begged to go too.

"Watch out for your feet then," Nökkina said.

"Perhaps we too should do a bit of exploring," said Dovergubben as they watched the troll babies scamper away. So each pair set off in a different direction, agreeing to meet back in Troll Meadow at dusk.

Now if you should go exploring around Little Lake, you would find all sorts of animals there—bear, elk, deer, rabbits, and bushy-tailed foxes both silver and red. Garter snakes, water snakes, toads and frogs go ambling along the forest floor. And out on the river rocks, you might even spot a lizard, dozing in the noonday sun. Overhead, the birds are too many to count—robins, warblers, thrushes, finches, golden eagles, ouzels, osprey...

It was chipmunks that the troll babies first encountered. There are no such creatures in Norway, you see, so when the troll babies saw these fuzzy little animals, they chased them from stump to stump, trying to get a closer look. The chipmunks chortled and scampered all about, poking out of peepholes and egging the newcomers on.

But troll babies tend to forget how big they are. Kalvehalen came bounding off a log and landed with a crunch on a chipmunk's tail. To her horror, it broke off!

"Oh, it's no matter at all!" chattered the chipmunk. "It's got less feelings than your fingernails."

Kalvehalen was not convinced. The chipmunk was rolling and stumbling all over the ground. You see, the tail of a chipmunk serves many purposes. For one thing, it acts a bit like a rudder when the little fellow hops from log to log. For another, it steadies him like a parachute whenever he takes a flying leap through the trees.

Now, without it, the little chipmunk had lost all sense of balance. Tearfully, Kalvahalen carried it home to its mother.

The chipmunk mother didn't seem the least disturbed. "He'll grow a new one by and by," she chuckled. "And for now he won't keep scampering off!"

Still, Kalvehalen felt bad.

"You will feel much better if you have a little munch,"

comforted Rumpungen. "I spotted some huckleberries back there a way."

So off they set, and in no time they sniffed ripe berries on the wind. But what was this? Someone had already beaten them to the bushes, someone as big and hairy as they.

Apparently the animal heard their footsteps. "Come join me, brothers!" called a female voice, and the animal turned to face them.

She hadn't turned but halfway around when the troll babies realized this berry-eater was a bear! The bear was even more startled than they. They turned from each other and began to run. Then something made them glance back over their shoulders. Perhaps it was just that there was something rather friendly about looking so much alike from the rear. Whatever it was, they came sniffing toward each other, and before long they were sharing the same huckleberry bush.

"You've come to prime berry country," said the bear as she munched. "For besides Little Lake, there are many others—Bear Lake, Hum Lake, Duck Lake, Pearl Lake, and a big lake down south by name of Cascade.

"I wouldn't go down there, though," she advised. "There are too many humans, just as there are at the big lake in town."

Then she stood up and stretched her paws. "My name is Ursi," she said. "How'd you like me to show you around?"

The two tails flicked eagerly, but Nökkungen frowned at his feet.

"Good grief!" laughed Ursi. "I don't think you can go very far on land with *those*! Maybe you'd better hop on my back."

So Nökkungen did, and off they went, ambling along beside the river.

"If you're going to live here," Ursi said as they walked, "you'll have to learn what this land is all about—what you can eat and what you can't, what will protect you and what will hurt." Then she began pointing out all sorts of plants and explaining their uses.

"And here's my favorite!" she said, sniffing a little white flower. "It's called syringa."

"Syringa," repeated Rumpungen, somberly chewing it. "And what's its purpose? What's it good for?"

"Good for? Why, it's good for sniffing!" laughed Ursi.

"You know so much about this land," said Kalvehalen. "You must have lived here for a long, long time."

"Oh, yes," said the bear. "I've lived here with my parents ever since I was born last spring."

The troll babies gaped. Born just last spring? Ursi hardly looked like a baby! How could she be so wise, if she was so much younger than they?

Just then there was a rustle in the bushes. Deep in the leaves, two eyes suddenly flashed, peering out from behind a black mask.

"A bandit!" yelped Nökkungen, grabbing Ursi's fur.

Ursi laughed. "That's just my friend Procie! Calm down!"

Then as the fellow padded out, Nökkungen began to giggle. "No wonder you're friends with him, Ursi!" he said.

"Sure, I crack fresh water mussels for her," Procie boasted. "But why are you laughing? Am I so funny?"

"No, but in Norway you're two of a kind, for the humans call you *vaskebjörn!*" Nökkungen giggled. "*Vaske* means 'wash' and *björn* means 'bear.' Washbear!"

Procie winced a little. "Humans!" he said. "What names they call us! The Indians named me *arahkun*, which means 'hand scratcher,' of all things! But I like 'Procie;' at least it's got some dignity, and there's even a star named for me!"

The shadows were lengthening, and the troll babies knew their mothers would soon start worrying that they'd turned to stone. "Farvel!" they called to the pair.

Back in Troll Meadow the others were gathering. "Guess what we saw!" called the troll babies as they raced in. Tumbling all over each others' words, they told of the chipmunk and the two "björn."

"You think you saw something!" said Langemann. "Your mother and I met an elk in the forest. He told us his name is Alces, and we told him about Troll-Elgen in Norway."

"Ja, but he's another one who thinks he's a moose!" laughed Nesa.

"Well, we met a beaver named Castor," said Nökken. "All through the lake he showed Nökkina and me, and kindly introduced us to each of the fish."

A groan swept through the gathering.

"Ah well," sighed Jotulen. "Plenty of mushrooms there are! A little grouse on the mountain showed us which ones are good."

"And also she showed us a cave," beamed Kari, "that will make a fine home for us and our little one."

All this time Fosekallen had been trying to get a word in, but when he finally got the chance, all that came out was stuttering. Surely this had to be news indeed, for the trolls couldn't understand a word he said!

Finally he managed to get it out. "Th-that little ouzel showed me the river. Like mine, her feathers are soft and strong. This winter I will teach her to walk under water, just l-like we do back home in Norway."

"Well," smiled Dovergubben, "what is her name?"

"F-f-fosina!" Fosekallen stammered.

How the troll babies snickered! For *fosina* only means "a girl Fosekallen;" and they knew the little troll had made the name up. Now they laughed and pointed at poor blushing Fosekallen until he turned into a bird and hid in Dovergubben's hair.

"That's enough," Dovergubben scolded them. Then he turned to the others. "Ja, it seems we have found a few friends. But still I wonder if they will object to our trolldom."

"Why, how could they," Grandmother Kjerringa burst in, "when they see all that trolls can do for a forest? We must hold a *velkomstfest* so they can get a feel for our ways."

At that, all the others started talking! Perhaps the celebration could be that very night! But Dovergubben shook his head. "Tonight we must sleep, for such things take preparation," he said.

"Then tomorrow night?" pleaded little Nökkungen.

Dovergubben grinned. "All right," he said. "Tomorrow night."

That night the wind blew softly around Little Lake, but the trolls' dreams were tossed and restless. Tomorrow night would be the velkomstfest, but not until they felt as one with the forest could this land really be their trolldom. No, not until they felt truly accepted would they be able to call it Trollhaven.

All through the next day, a certain tension hung on the air, almost like the sixteenth of May. For hours, the trolls had been making preparations, and now, toward evening, they gathered in Troll Meadow.

They looked around at the food they had collected—honey for Ursi, mussels for Procie, the tenderest willow shoots for Castor the beaver. There were elderberries, serviceberries, huckleberries, strawberries, watercress, mushrooms, and shoots of mountain ash. Who could turn down such a feast?

They had been inviting animals all day long. But would they come? For even in Norway, trolls and animals meet separately, a custom which nobody ever bothered to explain. Wasn't it natural that they all meet as one? Perhaps here in the New World things could be different; after all, they shared the same surroundings. At least the trolls *hoped* the animals would be willing to share!

Darkness came and the woods began to stir. Shadows flickered at the edge of Troll Meadow. There were twitchings and rustlings and sniffings. The trolls waited.

The animals were definitely approaching, but they hung back at the edge of the meadow. Not a one wanted to be the first to enter. A few had gathered around Alces, the elk.

"You first," whispered a white-tailed deer.

"No, him," replied Alces, indicating a mule deer buck.

No one moved.

Now others were coming up the forest path—Castor the beaver and the grouse with her children. The magpie and raven flew down from Jughandle, while herons and ouzels flocked in from the river. Ducks, marmots, ermine and lizards were making their way through the grass to Troll Meadow. Then Ursi arrived with Procie and his family, who in turn had invited Mephit the skunk.

"Only don't get too excited," Ursi warned Mephit, or you'll end this party before it begins!"

Now came all the chipmunks of the forest, for Kalvehalen had invited every last one. They in turn had invited the ground squirrels, who'd invited the pine squirrels, who'd invited the muskrats, who'd invited the foxes. And one red fox had rather slyly invited himself four Canadian geese. Finally came Eret, the slow-moving porcupine. He hesitated, then carefully advanced. For once in his life, no one moved away.

Still they stood waiting at the edge of the meadow for someone to make the first move. At the very outskirts, Lepus the rabbit trembled. Why, here were gathered all the enemies of the forest. And beyond, in the clearing, he could spot the newcomers. What did it mean? What did they have in store?

"Well, what are we waiting for?" snorted Ursi. And with a bound she headed into the meadow.

The animals followed her, but kept close together and stopped just inside the clearing. Why, the newcomers were dancing! The animals stared. Such a gentle dance they had never seen. It seemed like water moving on a lake, opening in a ring that grew wider and wider. Finally the circle was as wide as the meadow itself.

"It's as if they have put their arms around us," whispered Mephit to Eret.

"*Velkommen!*" said Dovergubben. Then he blushed a bit. "No, I must not say that, for it is to *your* home we've come. Over ice fields, tundra and peaks have we traveled, always at the call of a dream. Now the wind seems to say this is the place, but it can be only if you say so too."

A murmur spread among the animals. Heads cocked. Eyes glanced warily about. Then Alces stepped forward.

"The land's not to give or take," he said simply. "What comes comes, what stays stays. And whatever dances is always welcome!"

As if on cue, two foxes leaped up. Standing on their hind feet, they patted front paws and began prancing round and round in circles. A grouse beat time, a Canadian goose honked, and one by one the others joined in the music-making.

Soon Procie himself started to dance, then Alces, Lepus, and Eret the porcupine. Then to the trolls' delight, a grey heron stepped in, just like the cranes back home in Norway. More and more joined the dance, each in his own way, until even the trees seemed to sway along. Ursi rocked to and fro with little Nökkungen straddling her back.

Now the dance grew fast and furious. "Ursi! Ursi!" called the troll baby as they whirled. "You are like the great bear Valdermon back in Norway! Your fur is silky and soft as his, and it keeps my hands warm!"

On and on they danced. But troll babies will be troll babies! All this time, Rumpungen had been twitching his tail. Why did Nökkungen always get all the rides? With a flying leap, he aimed for Ursi's back—but he missed and landed on Eret instead! Eret himself didn't particularly mind, but you can be sure that Rumpungen did! His wailing yowls finally brought the dancing to a halt.

"No matter," panted the animals. "We've danced our-

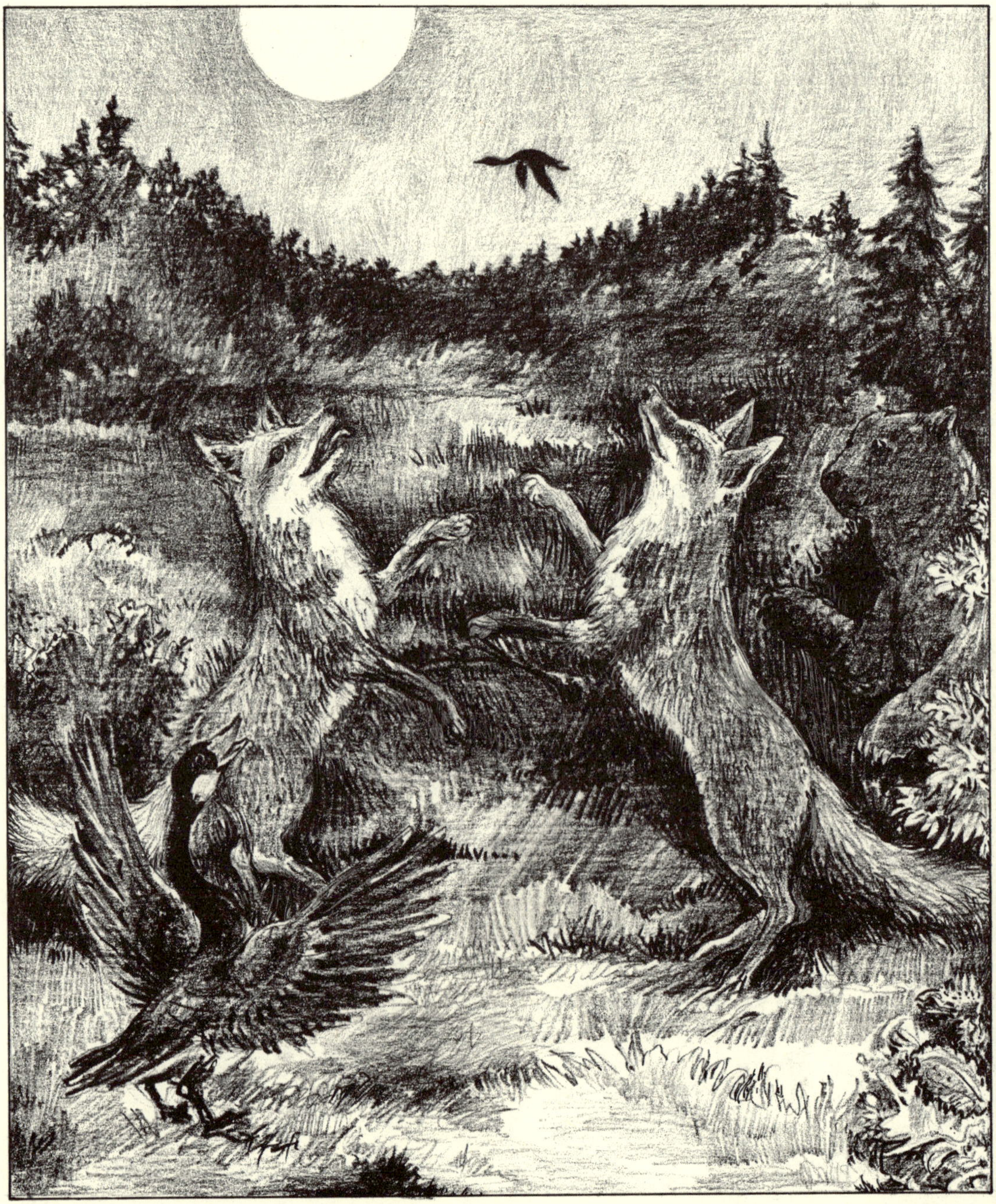

selves out anyway!"

Then while Langemann tended to Rumpungen's rump, the animals lay themselves down in a ring. For the first time since any of them could remember, none felt the least like chasing anyone. Even the goose who was nearest the red fox reached out with her long neck and gave him a nuzzle.

Suddenly their noses began to twitch. The trolls were bringing out the food. Such a feast it was, and all their favorites! Like any guests, they were a bit shy at first, but politeness and hunger don't mix very well. Soon everyone was lapping up the fruits of the forest. And if any of the earlier tension remained, you can be sure the last of it was gobbled up too.

Finally they all lay back, eyes half closed. "All that is missing now is the humans," sighed Dovergubben.

The animals stared.

"Humans!" snorted Alces. "Humans have no place here!"

"Surely one does," said Nökkina. "A white-haired one...?"

"Ah, the old one!" murmured many of the animals.

"Yes, you're right," Alces said to Nökkina. "Him we know well. He takes other humans into the high country and teaches them the ways of the woods."

"That's how we know our names," explained Procie. "We hear what he calls us when he talks of us to the humans."

"But he also talks to us of them!" chucked a chipmunk.

"And especially when we go fishing!" boasted the osprey. "In fact, he's even told us of trolls."

"Of trolls!" the trolls gasped. "What did he tell you?"

"Oh, that you might come here," answered the osprey.

"And he's told us lots of other tales, too, like the time in Norway when he was rescued by a troll."

The trolls sat upright. "Tell us!" they urged.

"It seems," the bird began, "that as a little boy out looking for adventure, he once spied an enormous tree. Something inside him just itched to climb, it, and so he did—right to the very top. Oh, it was ever so fine up there, he said. But when he started down, suddenly everything looked different. The ground seemed so very far away, he was terrified he was going to fall. He started whimpering and then began to cry, louder and louder, making the whole tree shake!

"Now it just so happened that tree was really a troll . . ."

"A troll?" the trolls interrupted. Something had stirred in their memories, something Storegubben had told them long ago. "And what did the troll do?" they asked eagerly.

"Why he took the boy home, of course," said Alces. "He walked to the boy's house at the edge of the forest, where he bent over and lowered him gently down to his mother."

"That's one reason the old one is so fond of trolls," chucked the mother of the little chipmunk who'd lost his tail. "He has always said there was something missing here."

But before the trolls could ask any more about this man, a pale rim of light began to outline Jughandle Mountain.

"*Ee-da-how*," murmured all the animals, and with small nods of farewell, they began to slip off through the trees.

The trolls could barely answer back. Ah, who would want it all explained? Right now it was enough to feel at home with the animals. But, they wondered, would they feel the same about the humans?

Touched by a Tail

Cool breezes now swept the meadow grass, and each night the trolls grew more familiar with the forest. Quite an active place it was, too. Besides the animals, they often saw humans, usually with rucksacks on their backs. The trolls came to recognize them as they followed the white-haired man—Carolyn, Carl, and the mother named Ann, who walked with her children, Holly and John. Sometimes the doctor or the tall girl followed, and sometimes there were several more. They always passed Little Lake on their way to the hills.

And when their friend wasn't leading a pack trip, he would come to Troll Meadow to sit with them around the fire. How he loved to listen to the trolls' tales! It turned out that he too was an expeditioner and had traveled the lands they had just passed through. Had they seen the musk oxen? Were the sad-eyed lemmings still there? Had the foxes shown them the weather station called Revesmuget? When they told him, how his eyes sparkled!

"Over three thousand miles! And in only ten months!" he marveled. "What a shame when such tales go unsung!" Then he chuckled a bit. "If only *National Geographic* had known!

But I wonder what they would have made of the okpiks!"

"Okpiks! You have seen okpiks?" cried the trolls. "But we thought humans couldn't see such things!"

"Why, all we need to do is open our eyes!" laughed their friend. "Tell me, why should Norwegians see trolls but not Sasquatch? Or Eskimos see kiwitaks but never a troll?" He shook his head. "Humans," he sighed, "one race as blind as another."

From these talks the trolls grew curious about the other humans who came to the lake. These strangers particularly interested Nökken, for often they fished above his home. Sometimes one would bring a loud motorboat or leave trash heaped along the shore. This always troubled Nökken. He could sense how the trees shrank from the noise, and the bitterness of the lake as it lapped a can.

Yet most nights Little Lake was peaceful, and Nökken would float quietly beneath the moonlit waves. Often he spied the doctor out strolling the forest paths, or the white-haired man leading backpackers home from the hills. Nökken also loved to watch the pranks of the three troll babies.

You see, they were so anxious for the humans to *believe* that they scampered after them and tugged on their clothes. The doctor would spin around and find huckleberries in his pockets, and the tall girl would gasp to find daisies in her hair. But the funniest of all was when Ann's son John found a mountain of worms in his fishing hat!

Nökken chuckled. If only they knew how to open their eyes!

Then one night, as he floated in a moonspot, he woke to feel rocks hitting his belly.

"Cut that out, Jotulen!" he snapped, thinking the mountain troll must be nearby, scratching.

But a human voice answered. "Forgive me, Nökken! You looked like the moon itself!" It was the white-haired man. He trudged down to the shore and sat on a log.

"Do you always throw rocks at the moon?" Nökken asked.

"Only when I'm frustrated! You should see what they're doing!"

"Who?" Nökken asked.

"Oh, the people," groaned the man. "Today I finished my trips for the season and moved to a cabin on the outskirts of town." He stopped and took a swig from his flask. "But you should see it! They're cutting down trees, leveling the ground, and building on every bare spot they make!"

"Surely not all of them!" Nökken objected.

"No," sighed the man. "Only a few, I suppose. And some are even trying to make things better—put in a park, clean up the big lake. But the rest just sit back and don't seem to see."

"Americans!" Nökken clucked up at the moon.

"Americans?" choked the white-haired man. "No! Some are Norwegians! Some are Danes, Finns, Swedes! And don't tell me they're not doing the same in Oslo!"

He took another swig. "Ah, maybe that's why I go to the hills, so I can talk of trolls and try to forget."

"You talk of trolls to your hikers?" Nökken asked.

"Of course. Round the fire they love to hear of nothing else!"

The man paused. "And I think that, slowly, a few are beginning to see."

"Trolls?" asked Nökken.

"Well, at least something they haven't seen before," mused the man. "Especially that young one, the boy named John."

And so the next day Nökken wasn't completely surprised when the white-haired man brought John down to the lake. They came ambling along, carrying their fishing poles, and soon were standing on the shore.

"They are quiet trolls," the man was saying. "In Norway they are called Nökken or Nökkina, and they are known as the protectors of all the lakes."

Just then something caught Nökken's eye. As the man and boy cast their lines into the lake, the branches over their heads quietly parted. Down dangled two long troll baby tails. John didn't notice, so intent was he on catching a fish. And if the white-haired man noticed, he pretended he didn't.

But Nökken squinted. He seemed to remember an old Norwegian song:

O if ever you're touched by the tail of a troll,
You'll suddenly see them wherever you go . . .

SWISH! The tails brushed through John's hair. He dropped his rod.

"What did you say lake trolls look like?" he asked.

"Look for yourself," was all the white-haired man said.

Under the water, Nökken smiled and brushed a fish from the man's hook. The boy's eyes seemed to follow his every move.

For a long time the two humans fished in silence.

"And now, I have something to tell *you*," said John at last. "Did you know there's a serpent in the big lake in town?"

Both Nökken and the man perked up.

"Yes," the boy whispered. "Its name is Sharlie."

Then, as Nökken floated closer, John began to tell a story. According to the children in town, a great sea serpent lived in the lake. It had five humps, long slimy scales, and was about the same color as the logs that floated by the lumber mill.

"Of course, nobody knows if it's a boy serpent or a girl serpent. So that's why we named it Sharlie," John continued.

Nökken flicked away another fish. He strained his ears.

"And have you yourself seen it?" the man asked. Then, without waiting for an answer, he pulled in his line. "Let's try fishing somewhere else," he said. "Lake trolls! Sometimes they do their job just a little too well!" And away they went, taking the unfinished tale with them.

"Stewed in my own juice!" swore Nökken.

But what was this tale the children told? Was this serpent something a troll might see? All day long the tale bewitched him, until finally he could stand it no more. At sundown he set off for town.

All was still by the time he arrived, and because his feet were sore from the walk, he sat down to rest on a dock by the lake.

"Sharlie! Sharlie!" he called into the night. "Sharlie, are you there?"

Nothing answered. Again he called. It seemed that if any serpent did live out there, it certainly wasn't about to let Nökken know.

Well, there was one way to find out! SPLOOSH! Nökken was gliding under the water. Spots of moonlight helped him pick out objects along the bottom—oil drums, engine parts, bottles and cans.

"How sad you are, lake," Nökken murmured. The murky water stung his eyes, but still he swam. Still there was no sign of Sharlie.

"Perhaps this serpent's only a legend, like the meat-eating horse of Bear Island," thought Nökken.

He reached the Narrows and finally Cougar Island, but here the water was so very deep that even he, the great lake troll of Norway, was afraid to dive down.

Slowly the moon slipped behind a cloud. Then like a well of ink, everything went black! Winds whipped through the water! Waves crashed! And without a warning, Nökken was floundering for his life! He gasped, he choked, and when he finally surfaced, he was staring into two enormous eyes!

"What kind of trash fish are you?" rasped a voice.

"No fish am I. I am a troll," Nökken said bravely.

"Are trolls good to eat?"

"Terrible!" said Nökken.

"Great!" hissed the voice.

And suddenly a double row of teeth flashed in Nökken's face. "Why, surely you're Sharlie!" he managed to gasp.

"Surely you're Sharlie! Surely you're Sharlie!" the voice mocked. "That's the funniest thing I've ever heard!"

Now Nökken could see five humps shaking the surface, and then the laughing face of the monster itself!

"So you're the voice that was calling!" it said. "And here I thought it was just another drunk. They're the only folks who believe in me, you know."

"And the children," Nökken reminded.

"Kids!" snorted Sharlie. "Thirty years I've lived here, and

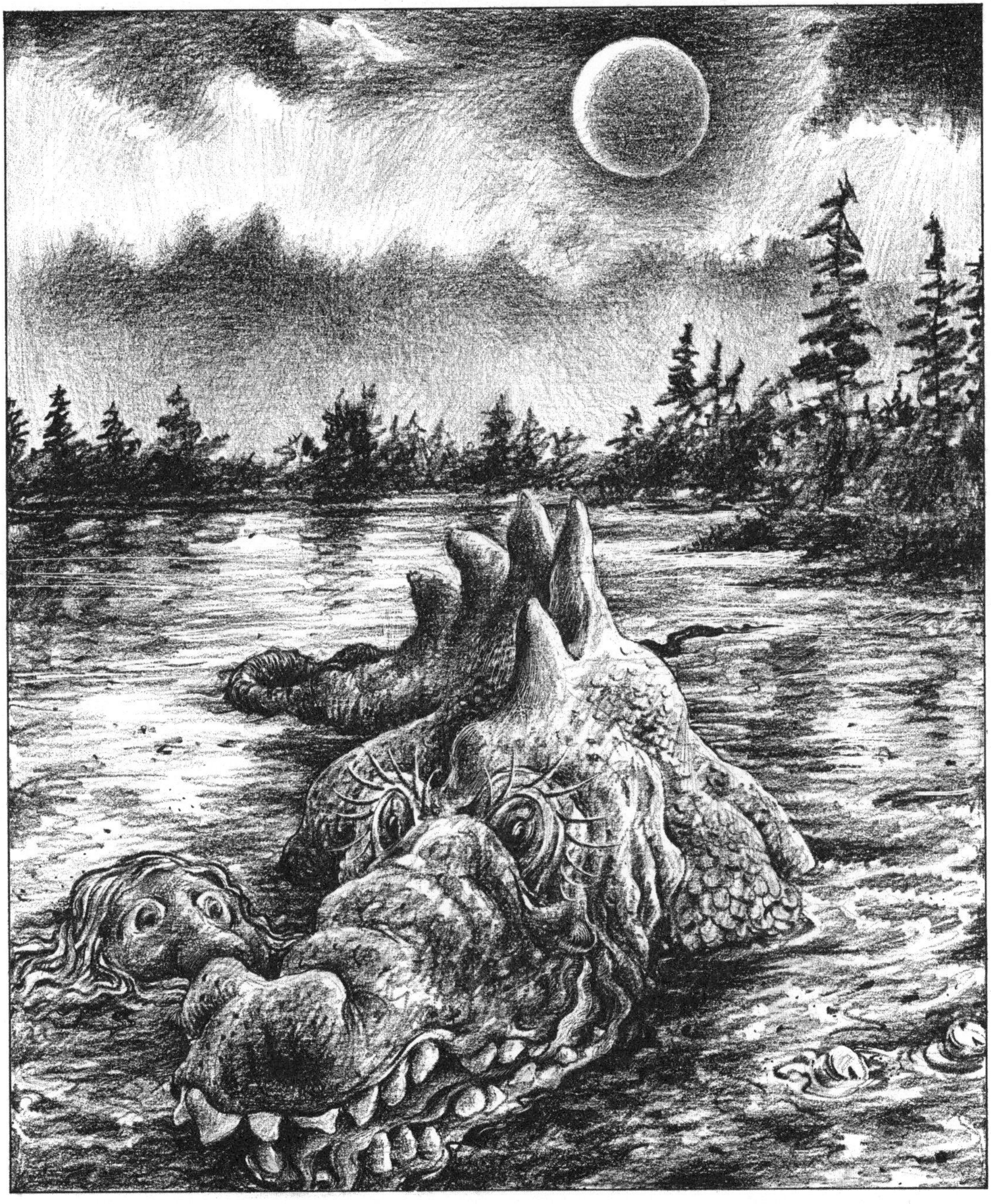

still the townsfolk say I'm a log."

"But were you always so big?" Nökken asked.

"Good grief, no!" Sharlie snorted. "At first I was just a little fellow. But when no one noticed me, I started to eat. I ate everything and anything they threw in the lake. And the more they threw, the more I ate."

"You mean you eat garbage?" Nökken groaned.

"The best!" said Sharlie. "But what good does it do? Big as I am, I still can't make them see me."

The serpent flicked its tail toward the lake troll. "Hang on!" it invited. "I'll show you my pantry!"

So Nökken grabbed the slimy tail and under they went. Never had the troll seen such a storehouse! On every shelf and sandbar was enough to feed a whole slither of serpents: buggies, bedsprings, broomsticks, bumpers; tools, tables, tires, timber . . .

"And that's only half of it!" Sharlie said when they surfaced two hours later.

But Nökken had grown to like this gruff creature, and what he had just seen troubled him. "I can't believe all that junk food could be good for anybody, not even a slimy serpent," he said. "What you need is a vegetable diet. Why not come live with me in Little Lake?"

Sharlie winced. "I think I'd rather eat here," the serpent rasped. "As long as they keep throwing more and more stuff into the water, I'll go right on eating more and more, until I'm so big that I fill the whole lake. *Then* maybe they'll see me!"

"And is that what you want most of all? To be seen?"

"Is that so very much to ask?"

Nökken shook his head.

"Doesn't every creature want to be seen for what he is?" Sharlie sighed.

Nökken nodded in agreement, but the serpent had already slithered back under the waves.

"Time for my midnight snack!" called the voice. "Be sure to come back before the lake freezes over!"

Nökken promised he would. Slowly he paddled back to the dock and then set out for home. Sharlie's words echoed through his thoughts. *Is that so very much to ask? Doesn't every creature want to be seen for what he is?*

When he finally arrived back at Little Lake, he again found the white-haired man throwing stones.

"Now what is it?" Nökken asked.

"The doctor!" The man threw another stone.

"The doctor?"

"Tonight we took a walk," he began. "After a while we came upon Kari. 'This is Kari,' I said. 'She's expecting a baby.' 'Since when do boulders give birth?' he laughed. And then he told me I'd better lay off my wine."

"Hmph!" grumped Nökken. "What is it with humans?"

"Ah, I should know better," sighed the white-haired man. "I forget they have to clear away years of cobwebs before they can manage to truly see."

"But not children!" Nökken winked. "Good news! John was right!"

"About the serpent?"

"There's a Sharlie, all right!"

The white-haired man tossed a rock to the sky. "I knew it! I knew that boy could see!" he cried. "And now I must get him an appointment with the doctor!"

Autumn Turns

White fog now hung over Little Lake each morning, like a veil enclosing a secret world. Then as the sun grew warm, the veil would gradually lift, leaving trails of frost on the sleeping trolls.

Not until sundown did the trolls get up. Sometimes they would see John walking with the doctor or fishing with another of the white-haired man's friends. Where the boy's eyes traveled, so did the others', watchful, eager, always expectant.

For the trolls, life went on as usual. Something about the forest was beginning to feel very much like a trolldom, but still they were cautious about naming it Trollhaven. For Storegubben had said it should be a home away from home, and still it seemed that something was missing.

Meanwhile, they explored with Ursi, helped Castor drag logs, and kept trying to convince Alces he was an elk, not a moose. One night Nökken took the others to the big lake to meet Sharlie, and after that one or another of them would go into town from time to time to pay the serpent a visit. Sharlie's cantankerous ways had them bewildered at first, until they learned the creature so looked forward to seeing them that it waited up for them every night.

Yet how quickly time passed! One day Ursi looked up at the trees. "I don't know what it is," she said, "but something tells me I should nose around a bit."

Then as they all looked up, they noticed a change in the leaves. The aspen, willow, cottonwood and tamarack were no longer quite as green as before. Even the mountain ash trees on Nesa's nose were hung with berries of an orangish hue. Procie and Ursi had begun to root around in the brush. The trolls glanced at one another. Was it really that time already?

Later that day, Nökken and Nökkina began moving their home. With Castor's help they had found a sheltered inlet where the lake would not be so likely to freeze. In the woods Dovergubben and Kjerringa were gathering pine boughs, while Langemann and Nesa moved a bit further inland from the river and its bridge. You see, a troll's nose grows longer with happiness, and now Nesa's needed more room.

Of course Jotulen and Kari were busiest of all, lining their cave with cattail fluff.

Only Fosekallen made no preparations. By now he had grown to know his little ouzel friend quite well. She even let him call her Fosina, but of course that couldn't turn her into a troll. So Fosekallen spent most of his time as a bird. Day after day the two ouzels winged along the river, heedless of the growing chill in the air.

There was another change, too. Almost daily now the white-haired man came to Little Lake, and with him the tall girl. Sometimes they fished, and other times the girl brought paper and wrote rapidly as the white-haired man talked.

Now the trolls could not hear just what he said, but it seemed that he was telling a tale. Often he would trace a trail in the dirt, or gaze toward the trees with a faraway look. Then the girl would look puzzled and squint at where his gaze settled. She'd rub her eyes and sometimes shake her head. Still she kept writing, day after day.

All around, the hills brightened from green to gold. Ducks rose from the lake with water trailing their wings. In the woods the squirrels were gathering pinecones, their bushy tails flicking off the cold.

Only Fosekallen played on. Each night his music floated out across Troll Meadow, and deep in the woods Fosina would hear. Now Fosekallen didn't know it, but often the little lady ouzel would fly over his waterfall and perch on the opposite shore. She would sway to his song. How it haunted her! But it told of a life for which she could scarcely hope.

Inside the waterfall, Fosekallen would be thinking of Fosina, wishing she could someday turn into a troll.

And so the autumn drifted on, golden days of flitting together along the river's edge, dark nights alone with the river running between them. Then one day Fosekallen heard Fosina humming. It was the song of the waterfall, the song of his longing.

That night Fosina flew beside Fosekallen to the waterfall that he had made his home. Now if you wanted to find Fosekallen's house in the river, you'd look for a hollow that the current has carved in an enormous rock. As the water rushes over, it creates a miniature waterfall, the silvery curtain of Fosekallen's door. It was on this rock that the birds came to rest.

"Don't be afraid," whispered Fosekallen to Fosina. "As long as you *believe* it will work, it will! Now spread your wings and follow me."

Then straight into the waterfall he flew, and midway through turned into a troll. Inside the hollow he picked up his violin and very gently began to play. Outside, Fosina trembled. She stood on one leg and then the other. Still the haunting melody floated out to her. At last she could resist it no more. Spreading her wings, she flew through the silvery curtain to find Fosekallen. And, midway through, it happened! Through the magic of the North, Fosina turned into the loveliest troll lady Fosekallen had ever seen!

Fosina said nothing but sat down softly by his side. After a moment, Fosekallen began to play a new song. It was a song of the river flowing, of the quietness of the pools and lakes, and of the aspen that move gently in the autumn wind. It was a song of the snowfall, and sometimes it was simply the song of silence that you hear when you sit alone in the woods.

"At last," sighed Fosekallen, "I too am prepared for winter."

A few nights later, as the trolls were sleeping, a breeze came rustling the leaves around their ears. Suddenly there was a great roaring! Jughandle Mountain was rumbling like thunder! The trolls leaped up. An avalanche! An earthquake!

But what was this? It was only Jotulen, clattering headlong down the mountain. He stood there trembling like his own private earthquake, and by his bright eyes everyone knew what the great excitement was all about.

Fosekallen poked his head from the waterfall. "What's going on?" he asked.

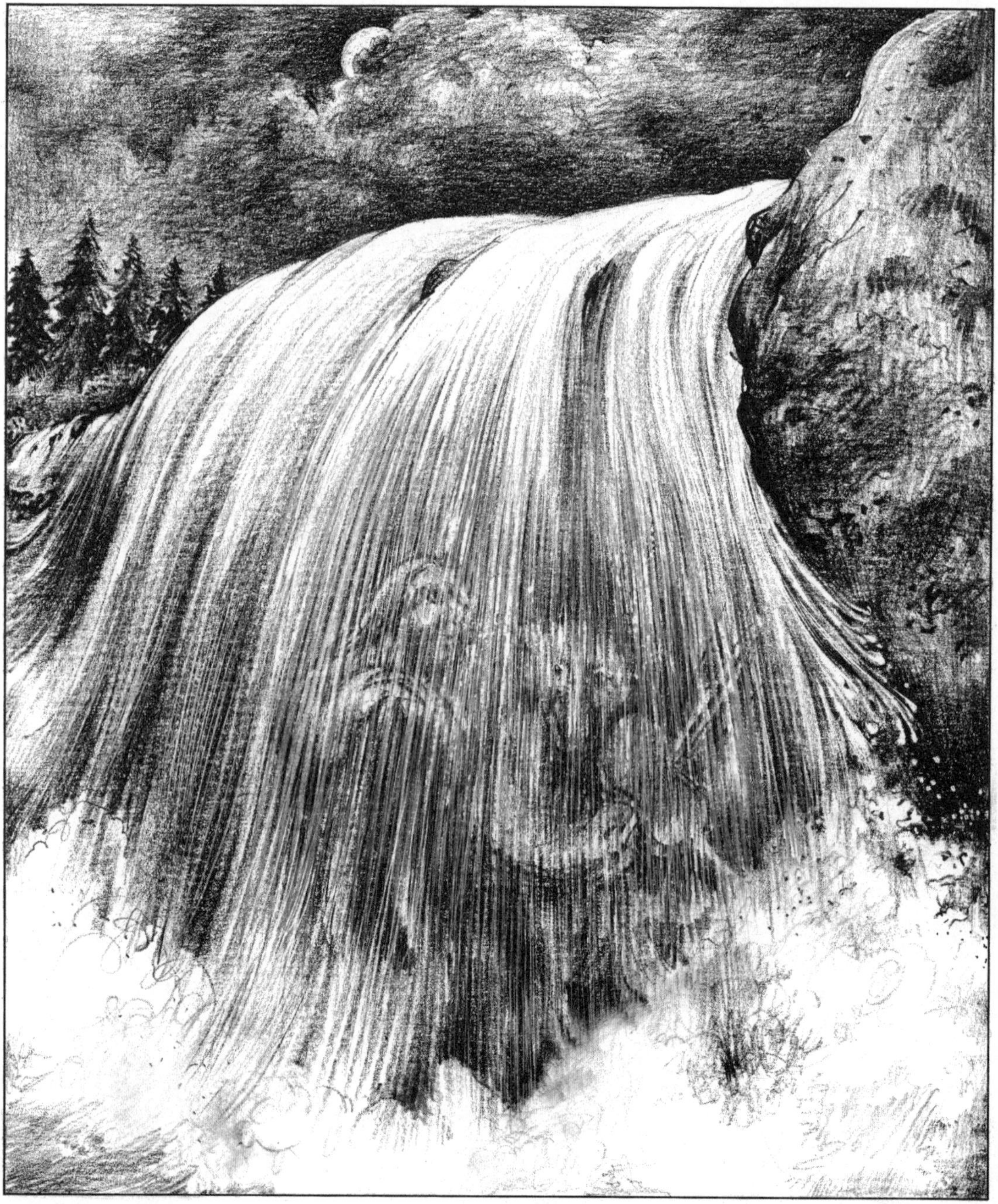

"K-K-Kari's up in the cave! About to have our b-b-baby!" stammered Jotulen. "She's doing fine—it's m-m-me that needs help!"

"Ha, that you do! And we shall come!" laughed Grandmother Kjerringa.

Then, throwing their arms around the mountain troll and one another, they all set out to climb Jughandle. All, that is, except Fosekallen and Fosina. Quickly they fluttered themselves into birds and flew together over the forest. "A troll baby! A baby troll!" they sang loudly. "The first troll ever to be born in America!"

They reached the cabin at the forest's edge and pecked noisily at the upper window. The white-haired man peered out.

"Kari's having her baby!" sang Fosina.

With a leap and a bound, the white-haired man was into his clothes and out the door. "We must get the doctor!" he called, straddling his bicycle.

"B-but trolls don't need doctors! You should know that!" cried Fosekallen, trying to keep up.

But the white-haired man kept right on peddling, until it was all the little birds could do to stay with him. Finally they landed, out of breath, on his shoulder. It never did any good to argue with him anyway!

When they reached the doctor's house at last, all the lights were out and the windows dark. Three times the white-haired man pounded. Then three times more. Finally the doctor appeared.

"What in the world . . .?" he mumbled sleepily.

"Wake up!" the white-haired man commanded. "For two

months, twelve trolls have inhabited your land! Last week a new one grew out of a waterfall, and tonight another is about to be born! It's high time you saw for yourself!"

The doctor groaned.

"Hurry!" urged the white-haired man.

"Hurry! Hurry!" sang Fosekallen and Fosina.

The doctor blinked at the two little birds. Finally he shook his head and shrugged. "Well, only because I can't refuse a house call," he grumbled.

As soon as he'd dressed and grabbed his black bag, they set off. Fosekallen led the way, but the mountain was slippery with frost, so the hike up Jughandle took longer than they expected.

Meanwhile, the trolls had gathered outside the cave. Inside, Jotulen was helping Kari, and Grandmother Kjerringa was helping Jotulen, who was trying hard to be less clumsy than usual and not succeeding at all.

The rest of the trolls waited silently in the dark. Their ears twitched. They could hardly stand still. At last they heard the lusty squeal of a troll baby. Their heads lifted. Their eyes brimmed with laughter. They hugged one another in the night. Then, when Jotulen gave the signal, they all tiptoed into the cave.

Now as all trolls know, whenever a baby is born—be it animal, troll, or human—something sets the air to vibrating. Perhaps it's when the waiting finally gives way to wonderment, but whatever it is, it can make you tingle all over!

And so, midway up the mountain, the doctor stopped. "I don't even need to see," he whispered. "The very night is ringing with it!"

Then with a whoop and a holler, the white-haired man went bounding up Jughandle so fast the other three could barely keep up. Outside the cave, he stopped short. "One thing you should know," he advised the doctor. "You can tell the health of a troll baby by measuring the length of its tail. The longer the tail, the healthier the baby. Just remember that if you examine this one!"

Then they tiptoed in. All around Kari were gathered the trolls, and in her arms was a fuzzy troll baby.

The doctor gasped.

"Would you like to hold it?" Kari beamed.

The doctor looked a little uncertain. For one thing, he didn't understand Norwegian. For another, he seemed to be having trouble with his eyes. He blinked and squinted. But as he did, Jotulen proudly handed the baby to him. It was three feet long and weighed about twenty-five pounds. It had pink ears, blue eyes, and a long furry tail.

Gingerly the doctor held out the tail: two feet . . . three feet. . . . He looked up and grinned. The trolls grinned back, even Jotulen, who for the second time in his life forgot all about his bad teeth. But it was Nökken whose grin was the widest of all, and as he watched the doctor he began to hum softly: *"O if ever you're touched by the tail of a troll . . ."*

"His name is Rolfus!" Jotulen announced. "O! Himmel! It is October thirteenth! This same day last year we set out for America!"

Then from far below came the sound of calling. The animals were gathering at the mountain's base. "Is the little one safe?" they called.

The trolls stepped out one by one and stood with Rolfus to

greet the dawn. Then such a joyful sound rang out as had never been heard before: bird song, squirrel song, the bugling of elk, and even a song from Lepus the rabbit, who hadn't known he had a voice!

The sound rose to the mountain and spread over the town, and deep in their sleep, a few humans heard it—Carolyn, Carl, and the mother named Ann, who heard Holly and John calling back to it in their dreams. In the house nearby, the Nelson family heard it and turned in their beds. The sound tickled the ears of Björn the Swede and fluttered the eyelids of the tall girl and her husband. Down to the south it roused Chris, Steve and the artist, and wakened Little Claire and Marty and Suzanne. To the north the lady named Sister heard it and rang a bell, though she wasn't sure why she did. Asleep or awake, all of them smiled at this indefinable sound that spoke so clearly of joy.

And they say, those who saw the light break over Jughandle, that it sparkled just a bit brighter that morning.

The Call of the Mountain

Clouds were drifting in from the west, alta stratus, drifting higher, becoming cumulous, the snow-bearers. For many days now the squirrels' chatter had hushed, and down by the river, Ursi curled in her den. Silence filled the forest, as if the trees were waiting for something.

Out on the lake, the geese would rise at dawn, circling slowly many times. The first few to fly were joined by others, until they filled the sky. Then, with a long cry of farewell, they would leave Little Lake, bound for warmer lands to the south.

Still the trolls saw the white-haired man come daily to the shores with the tall girl. Still she continued to write, though often now she paused to blow on her hands. They saw many of the other humans, too, hiking Jughandle or sitting on the lakeshore, waiting quietly, like the trees—always waiting, watching for something.

Then one day, tiny flakes fell from the sky, first a few, then more and more. All around, the trees seemed to reach out their branches, for they know that snow protects them and keeps them warm.

About a month after Rolfus's birth, the wind suddenly shifted from west to north. Now the snow crystals were no longer small. Large and fluffy, they fell by the hour, and deep in the woods the trolls knew winter had come. Even Fosekallen's rock was blanketed with snow, and thin icicles hung where water once rushed.

Now mountain trolls grow fast, and by mid-December little Rolfus was almost ten feet tall. Every night new snow fell from the sky, and every night the other troll babies thought up new games. You see, even though Rolfus was much bigger than they, they knew he was younger and eager to please. He joyfully rolled their snowballs for them and giggled when they rode him like a sled. He bounced among them, delighting in everything, rolling in the snow, jumping out of trees, and even taking dares to tickle Ursi as she napped in her den.

Then one morning Rolfus couldn't sleep. Something in the air kept nipping him awake, daring him to sneak out of the cave. Softly he left his mother and father and slid down Jughandle to Little Lake. But then he stared!

Little Lake had frozen into a solid field of ice!

For once Rolfus didn't go bounding, but instead sat gazing in wonder at the crystal world around him. Everything was blue and white and silver, and away in the distance Brundage Mountain sparkled like a sugar lump.

"What lies on top of that mountain?" Rolfus wondered.

And the more he gazed, the more he wondered. And the more he wondered, the more his nose itched until it sent quivers tickling down into his tail....

Early the next morning the white-haired man came skiing

up from the Nelsons' place. Overnight, a storm had covered the willows, and now they bent fairy-like over the river. He stopped and gently touched a branch.

Suddenly there was a great moaning, as though the earth were giving way beneath the snow. The white-haired man turned and raced off in the direction of the sound. It seemed to be coming straight from Troll Meadow.

Sure enough, when he arrived he found all the trolls clustered around Kari. All were in tears, and great heaps of ice crystals were gathering at their feet.

"Well, what is it? What's the matter?" asked the white-haired man.

"Our Rolfus is lost! Gone since last night!" cried Kari. "And nowhere can we find him!"

"O! Himmel! We'd better do something fast!" said the man. "Or you'll bury yourselves in frozen tears!"

So the trolls led their friend down to Little Lake to show him the spot where Rolfus had been sitting. Leading away from it, almost filled with new snow, were fat, round, troll-baby tracks, with a tail trail dragging between them.

"Why didn't you follow them?" asked the white-haired man.

"Last night we tried, but too far did they go," moaned Jotulen. "And this morning . . . Look how bright the sun! If we were to set forth, we'd turn to stone for sure!"

"Ah, don't worry," their friend comforted them. "Once long ago a troll saved me. Perhaps now I can help in return."

Then, reminding them to keep to the shadows, he skied off. Right across Little Lake went the tracks, then down the road and through Ponderosa Park. And there they ended abruptly, right at the edge of the big lake. It had not yet frozen.

The white-haired man lowered his eyes. What to tell Kari? How could he ever . . ."

But when he raised his head, he was staring right at Brundage Mountain. Like a sugar-coated diamond it glistened against the sky, like a star you might wonder at, like a sea that beckons, like a mighty tree you'd long to climb. . . . Like a *tree*!

Suddenly the white-haired man had a hunch. He squinted at the sunny mountain crest. There was no time to lose! Even if Rolfus hadn't drowned, there was a good chance he might be a rock pile by now!

"I'll have to have some help, though," the man thought. Straight to the tall girl's house he skied. He could see her in the window, typing at her table.

"Our book can wait!" he blurted as she opened the door. "Hurry! Get your coat and skis!"

"But I'm right in the middle of the birth of Rolfus!" she protested.

"Hurry! It's Rolfus himself who needs you now!" the man urged.

Then he ran into her house and grabbed her skis, and while he hurriedly waxed them, she pulled on her parka. In no time they were racing for Brundage Mountain.

"But I'm still not sure I can see . . ." she panted.

The white-haired man just kept going. Faster and faster they skied, then slower and slower as they headed uphill. All along the trail, the trees hung heavy with snow. Then just as they reached the Goose Lake turnoff, the tall girl suddenly stopped. "Look," she said, pointing with her ski pole.

The tree looked like a great white candle, slumped and softening in the sun. It stood about twelve feet high. One snow-covered branch stretched out strangely behind it, and the girl moved close to touch it. "Isn't this odd?" she said. "I never saw a branch grow quite like this."

"Very peculiar," said the man.

Suddenly a little snow fell from the tree, followed by a big splotch of water. The white-haired man looked up, and there, blinking down at him, was a big blue eye.

"Thank goodness it stormed last night and covered you," laughed the man. "Otherwise you'd be a rock pile for sure!"

Flicker . . . splotch! A second eye appeared.

"Your mother and father have been worried about you! For one thing, you're the first troll born in America!"

Still the huge snow mound said nothing; but another drop rolled softly down and landed—PLOP—on the tall girl.

"When it's dark you must hike back down the mountain, cross Little Lake, and not stop until you get home," directed the man.

"But I'm scared!" came a muffled voice.

"Come now, you can do it."

A torrent of tears fell from the mound.

"Oh, very well," comforted the man. "I'll take you down myself at dark." Then he turned to the tall girl. "You must . . ." he began.

But then he stopped, for the girl was staring wide-eyed at the troll baby, drenched from top to toe with his tears.

"He *is* there!" she gasped.

"Why, of course he is!" laughed the white-haired man.

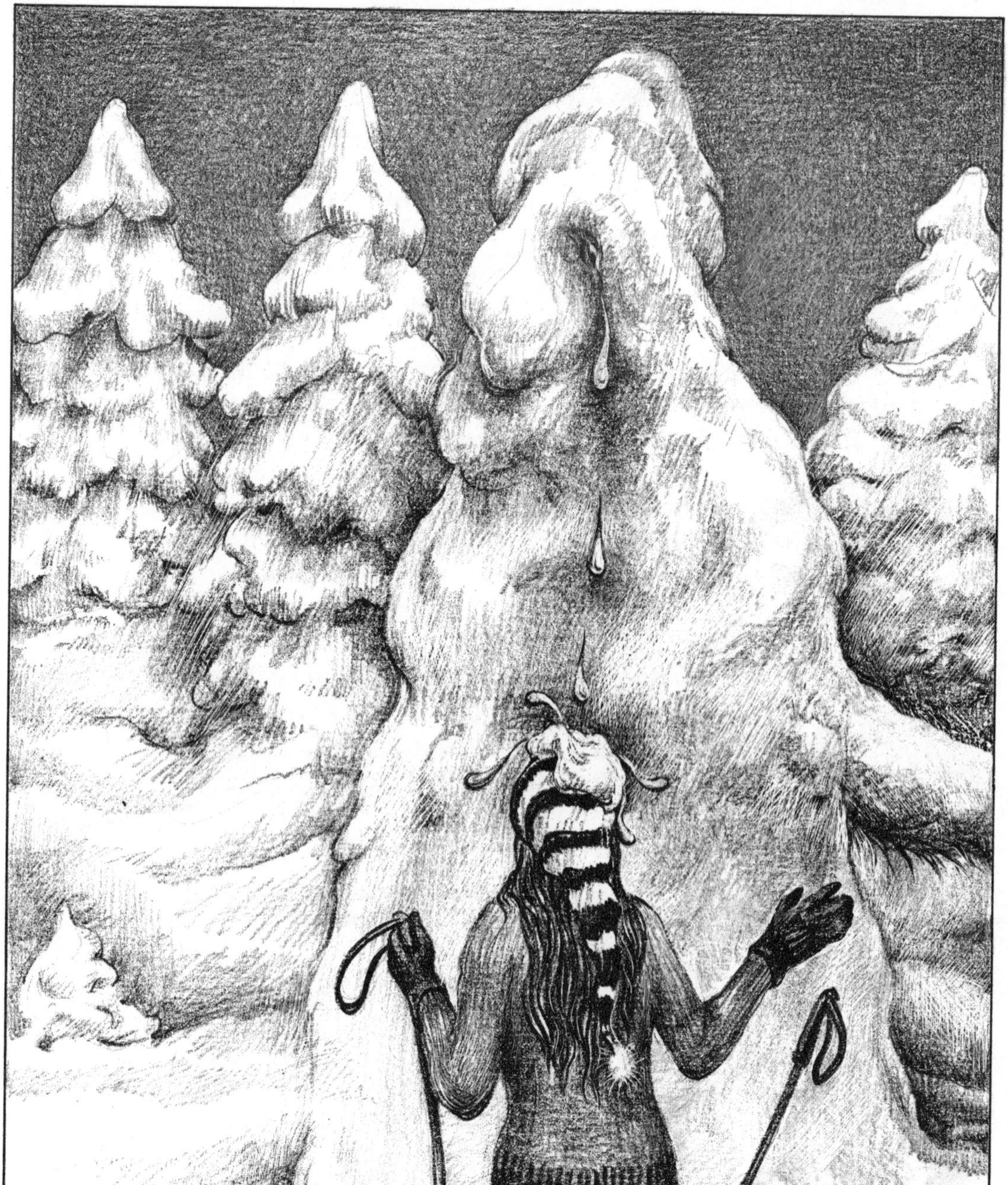

"You found him, and now you must hurry down to Troll Meadow! Tell them I'm bringing him home at dark!"

"But I can't speak Nor..."

"Hurry! They're worried!"

The girl gave a last, startled look over her shoulder as she planted her poles and pushed off down the mountain.

"Good work, Rolfus," chuckled the white-haired man. "I know you didn't set out to do it, but I do believe you've just made a friend for yourself, and maybe one for all the trolls. Now then, let's move into the shadows."

Then he began to brush off the troll baby's back. "Rolfus," he said as he swept off the snow, "let me tell you about seal-skin skis. The skis themselves are made of wood, but their bottoms are covered tightly with fur. Like yours, the hairs all point one direction, so when you ski uphill they catch in the snow and keep you from sliding backwards. But headed downhill, the hairs flatten and slide smoothly, and if they're waxed just right, you can fly like the wind!"

He pulled a bar of wax from his pocket.

"But I have no skis. And I'm scared to walk!" whimpered Rolfus. "Somebody's got to carry me!"

"Carry you!" laughed the man. "Don't you see? I'm going to wax you like skis and ride you down like a sled!" And with that he began waxing Rolfus's back.

Meanwhile the trolls had all fallen asleep under the trees around Troll Meadow. Noon had come with still no sign of their friend or of Rolfus, so at last, to escape their sorrow, they had taken refuge in sleep and dreams.

But even rest was no refuge for Kari. Nightmares rumbled through her sleep, dreams of ten-foot rock piles pitifully calling for help. And then, as she turned in the soft snow, it seemed something came to rest on her shoulder. Kari cracked open one eye. Why, it was the tall girl! She was sitting gingerly, as though she wasn't quite sure what rested beneath her.

"*God dag,*" said Kari.

The girl stood up. "I-I'm afraid I don't speak Norwegian," she apologized.

Kari smiled reassuringly. For unlike humans, trolls have no problem with language. They may not know what every word means, but they always manage to understand the message. So just as she might have understood a cricket or a chipmunk, Kari understood what the tall girl now said.

In a torrent of words, the girl poured out the story of how the white-haired man had found Rolfus on the mountain. "And he says they'll be home at sundown!" she finished.

Kari's eyes were glazed.

The girl clutched the troll mother's hands. "Did you understand?" she asked.

"Ja! Ah, *vidunderlig!*" Kari breathed and smiled.

But the girl frowned and shook her head at the word. "Vidunderlig?"

"Ja! Vidunderlig! Vidunderlig!" Kari laughed, spreading her arms wide to the sky.

The girl raised her head.

"Vidunderlig!" repeated Kari, giving her a hug.

The girl's face burst into a smile. "Ja! Vidunderlig! *Wonderful!*" she cried.

"Ja! Vonderfool!" Kari laughed.

For a moment the two stood grinning at each other. Then

the girl placed her hand on Kari's arm. "I must go now," she said. "But I'll be back here at sundown. Look for me. I'll be watching from the trees!" Then, with a wave of farewell, she skied off through the forest.

Dusk came and the dim winter sky grew dark. Anxiously the trolls gathered at the edge of Little Lake. The air was still. They watched for some sign, but saw only snow. They listened for a sound, but heard only silence.

"Could it be," thought Kari, "I so misunderstood?"

Then behind her she sensed a flicker of movement. She turned. There, among the shadows of the trees, one shadow seemed to be waving a bit. In fact, several other shadows didn't look like trees either, and though they stood still, they too seemed to wave.

"Ah," sighed Kari and raised her hand to wave back.

Just as she did, a shout rang through the night. There was a whoosh! and a spray of snow, and sailing across Little Lake came Rolfus! The white-haired man was lying flat on the troll baby's belly, hanging onto his feet and trying to steer. Laughing and hollering, they skidded to shore.

How the trolls shouted! Straight for those two pair of arms they went racing, then bumped and went sprawling in the snow. Head over heels they went rolling and tumbling, hugging Rolfus, each other, and the white-haired man.

Their laughter filled the forest and echoed back from the trees. And had you been standing among those in the shadows, surely you would have been laughing too!

The Magic Language

The night on Brundage Mountain might have taught Rolfus about fear, but it certainly hadn't taught him not to go wandering. Now everything fascinated him, especially the animal tracks, and he learned to follow them through the snow.

The short-long ones belonged to Lepus, the dragging sweeps were from Castor's tail, and the dainty flower prints were left by the foxes. But one night Rolfus came on some he didn't know. Bigger than any others they were, yet so light they barely sank in the snow. And what a strange shape!

Rolfus followed them deep into the woods. It was very dark. The tracks were filling with snow.

Suddenly firelight shone through the trees. In the glow, Rolfus could see a pair of basket-like shoes propped against a tree in the distance. Rolfus moved closer.

Why, it was the white-haired man! He was seated by his fire, snow blowing through his hair, smoke curling about his shoulders.

"Why aren't you home in your cabin?" asked Rolfus.

"In my cabin it's always the same," sighed the man. "But out here—out here it's forever new."

For a long while the two watched the trails of smoke.

"Rolfus," said the man at last, "I've been thinking of an expedition."

"An expedition?" beamed Rolfus.

"Ja, in the spring. Ever since I rode you down the mountain, my mind has been filled with all sorts of dreams. Dreams of icecaps, fjells and fjords, of okpiks, kiwitaks, fulmars and seals..."

Rolfus's eyes shone in the night. "I've heard my parents speak of such things."

"My work here's almost through," the man continued. "I'm finished teaching. Our book's nearly done. And besides, I'm getting a little too rooted to home."

"Not I," said Rolfus, his face all aglow. "How I should love to go exploring!"

A funny look crossed the white-haired man's face. "Rolfus," he said abruptly, "let me see your eyes!"

Obediently, the troll baby raised his head. He watched the man's eyes sparkle over the fire. Why, they were neither green, nor brown, nor blue, nor grey, but all four colors burnished gold! From them came a look so faraway, he almost didn't hear when the man whispered, "Ah, you too, Rolfus?"

What did he mean by that? All Rolfus knew was that he longed for adventure! "Please can I go?" he begged.

"On an expedition there's no place for whiners," the man scolded gently. "It's going to be a treacherous trip. First, I'll go back to the Great Slave Lake and there finish my study of the bald eagle..."

"And from there?" asked Rolfus eagerly.

"From there I may return to Norway, for I have a friend

there I've been wanting to see."

Rolfus tried to hide his tail. "I'm not such a baby anymore," he said.

"Oh, even I was a baby once," laughed the man. "Didn't you hear how I was saved by a troll?"

Rolfus shook his head.

"Ja," said the man. "And all through my boyhood I was friends with that troll. I'd run out to meet him in the woods, and he would show me the ways of the birds and animals. Once he asked me if I knew I had Viking eyes. He taught me to hear what he heard on the wind, and soon far-off places began to call my name."

"And the wind, does it still call you?" Rolfus asked.

"Of course," sighed the man. "Why else would I go?"

Rolfus looked into the fire. "I'd give anything to meet your friend," he whispered.

"Then," said the man, "you must ask your mother."

Rolfus couldn't believe his ears. "What?" he cried.

"Hurry! Run now. She'll be worried!" was all the man said.

So leaving his friend sitting in the woods, Rolfus ran back to Jughandle as fast as he could.

The trolls were delighted to hear of the expedition, but saddened at the thought of seeing the white-haired man go. As for Rolfus, they weren't quite sure.

"Perhaps we should let him go," said Jotulen. "By spring he'll surely be big enough."

"And st-strong enough, too!" piped Fosekallen.

But Kari sat silent.

"Ah Kari," Dovergubben said to her, "even you and Jotulen weren't so awfully grown up when first we set out from Norway. And Rumpungen and Kalvehalen were still just babies! Sure, they were a little pesky at times, but they helped us make friends all across the Arctic."

"And Rolfus is surely friendly enough!" added Langemann.

"Ja, but wise enough?" Kari murmured.

The other trolls glanced at one another. They knew Rolfus wouldn't have to be so wise, for the white-haired man had wisdom enough for both. No, the real question was: could Kari bear to let her baby go? They decided to wait and see.

In the meantime, Christmas was coming! Troll Meadow lay deep in snow, and all around ran delicate tracks, signs that a few birds still lingered on.

Among the trolls there was much talk of the trolldom, for through they were coming to feel quite at home, something still seemed to be missing. Could it be, they wondered, that what was missing was simply Christmas? The white-haired man had told them that when humans first move into a new house, it's often not until they've spent Christmas in it that it truly feels like home.

Well, whether or not the holiday could do this for their trolldom, Christmas would still be Christmas for the trolls!

But one special gift—a bag of healthy food for Sharlie— had to be delivered early, before the big lake froze over and the serpent was locked beneath the ice for the rest of the winter. So three days before Christmas the trolls set out with Sharlie's gift.

"Oh, let me go first!" Rolfus cried. "I will show you how I can lead an expedition!"

The trolls chuckled softly, so eager was this troll baby to prove himself, especially to his mother. Even Kari smiled a little as she said, "Ah, there's no harm. Lead the way, Rolfus!"

So one after the other they followed the troll baby across the lake. "See you on Christmas Eve!" they called to the animals on the shore.

Now the animals had been stirred by all this talk of Christmas, and most of all by the talk of something the trolls called a "juletre." From the excitement they understood that it must be a very special tree, one that had great meaning for the trolls. So, with a surprise in mind, they set out to find it.

It didn't take long. At the edge of Troll Meadow grew a tall spruce that they had often seen the trolls admire. It had a high crest and heavy branches all around, and it always sparkled in the morning sun. Surely this must be the juletre, they thought.

But what to do with it? They talked a great deal. Well, they could always start by brushing off the snow. Immediately half a dozen tails went to work. Soon there was so much scurrying and chattering that the noise woke up many of the winter-sleepers.

"What's all that racket?" Ursi grumbled, poking her head through a mound of snow.

Excitedly the squirrels pointed to the juletre. "It's a Christmas surprise for the trolls!" they chucked.

"Christmas?" yawned several of the other sleepers.

So the squirrels repeated a few snatches of troll talk about feasting and singing, and especially about dancing around the juletre. Suddenly the sleepers weren't sleepy anymore.

Perhaps they would get up and help for a while. After all, who can sleep through a troll celebration? They bumbled around, trying to wake up, trying to figure out what to do with the juletre.

But the little chipmunk who had lost his tail came up with the best suggestion. "Why don't we, the chipmunks and birds and smaller animals, all sit in it?" he chucked. "I think that would look awfully nice. And when the trolls return, you others can seat them on this side of the tree. That way when they look up to the sky, the North Star will be shining right over the top."

So for the next few days the animals kept the juletre well brushed, though they did decide to leave the icicles hanging.

Then, on Christmas Eve, just as the North Star was beginning to glow, they took their places—the larger animals around the base, the birds and small animals in the branches. They sat very still. They waited. Around them the icicles tinkled on the wind. Were the trolls coming? Had they made it to Sharlie's? What if Rolfus had gotten mixed up?

What the animals couldn't know, of course, was that just on the other side of the hill, the trolls were wearily plodding home. Sharlie had been delighted with their visit, and Rolfus had only led them off the track once. Well, not exactly off the track, just in a rather roundabout way. He had wanted to see the Christmas lights over the town.

Now even Rolfus was weary. The trolls plodded slowly after him through the snow. Oh why did they always try to do so much before Christmas! Here it was, Christmas Eve, and they hadn't even begun their own preparations! Typical! Typical!

"Maybe we should just sleep through this one," groaned Nesa.

But what was that? Bird song? Coming from Troll Meadow? They lifted their noses and sniffed the wind. Spring sounds in the middle of winter? They hurried over the hill.

Closer and closer the chirping drew them. At the edge of Troll Meadow they stopped.

They could see it. Its icicles sparkled silver in the moonlight. Just as the little chipmunk had said, the North Star was shining right over the top, and on every branch sat a small bird or animal. Ah, never had they seen such a juletre! They stood enchanted, listening to it sing, and only when the larger animals stepped forward did the trolls realize from whom it had come.

Their eyes filled with laughter. Their weariness fell away as the animals led them to the sparkling tree. Then trolls and animals formed a ring around it. Now the only sound was the sweep of the wind as it gently rocked the branches.

The animals cocked their heads. They seemed to be waiting for something.

Then came the sound of branches breaking, and into Troll Meadow strode a great elk.

"That must surely be Troll-Elgen," whispered Rolfus, wide-eyed with wonder.

"Silly!" hissed Kalvehalen. "*You* never saw Troll-Elgen. And besides, it's only Alces."

Alces it was indeed, but Alces with a strong, new look about him. Then, as he entered the circle around the juletre, something strange happened: suddenly all the animals were standing on their hind legs!

Alces walked slowly over to the mountain troll baby. "You are wise, Rolfus," he said. "You saw right away." He looked around at the others. "It took you trolls to convince me I'm not a moose—but it's only today that I know who I really am."

"Yes," said Dovergubben, "and high time, too, for we need your advice, Troll-Elgen. You have heard of the white-haired man's expedition?"

Troll-Elgen nodded.

"You have heard that Rolfus wishes to go?"

The great elk nodded again.

"And what do you think?"

"Rolfus has proved himself both wise and strong," said Troll-Elgen. "But the decision is really Kari's."

But Kari didn't need to speak. Her smile told Rolfus all he wanted to know. "Mange takk, Mamma!" he cried. "O tusen takk, Troll-Elgen!"

"Shhh!" hushed Grandmother Kjerringa. "Listen!"

It seemed to them that they could hear music far in the distance, very faint.

"Could it be bells?" whispered Fosina.

"Or perhaps singing?" whispered Nesa.

All at once the trolls remembered the music they had heard one year before, on Spitsbergen.

"Ja, it *is* singing!" Kalvehalen breathed.

And it was coming closer! Far back in the trees, a golden glow appeared. Nearer it came, nearer and nearer, with the singing growing fuller all the time.

"It's the humans," somebody whispered.

Was it?

Then over the snow came shadows on skis, each bearing a burning torch. Many of the animals started to run, for to them humans and fire meant danger at its worst. But Dovergubben motioned them to stay.

One by one their faces came into view. There were Carolyn, Carl, and the mother named Ann, whose torch lit the faces of Holly and John. In the glow the Nelson family appeared, and the tall girl and her husband followed. Brighter and brighter the procession grew as Björn the Swede led the people from the south—Chris and Steve and Little Claire, the artist and the couple named Marty and Suzanne. Their lights shone on the lady named Sister, and behind, in her light, came the doctor. Finally through a tunnel of torchlight skied the white-haired man himself.

"Velkommen!" said Dovergubben.

For a moment the humans looked a little uncertain. Then Dovergubben motioned them into the ring. Torches were set softly in the snow as trolls and animals moved to make room.

So there they were! Trolls, animals and humans, together at last!

"Well, what are we waiting for?" bugled Troll-Elgen. And with that he slowly began circling the juletre. Some joined hands and others linked tails, and soon they were all circling round and round.

Livelier and livelier grew their steps. Then Fosekallen drew his bow, and the circle swung wide open. Over the snow they leaped and danced. Now, with Fosina by his side, Fosekallen played as never before! Like young trolls, old Dovergubben and Grandmother Kjerringa clasped hands and went whirling in and out among the trees. The young trolls

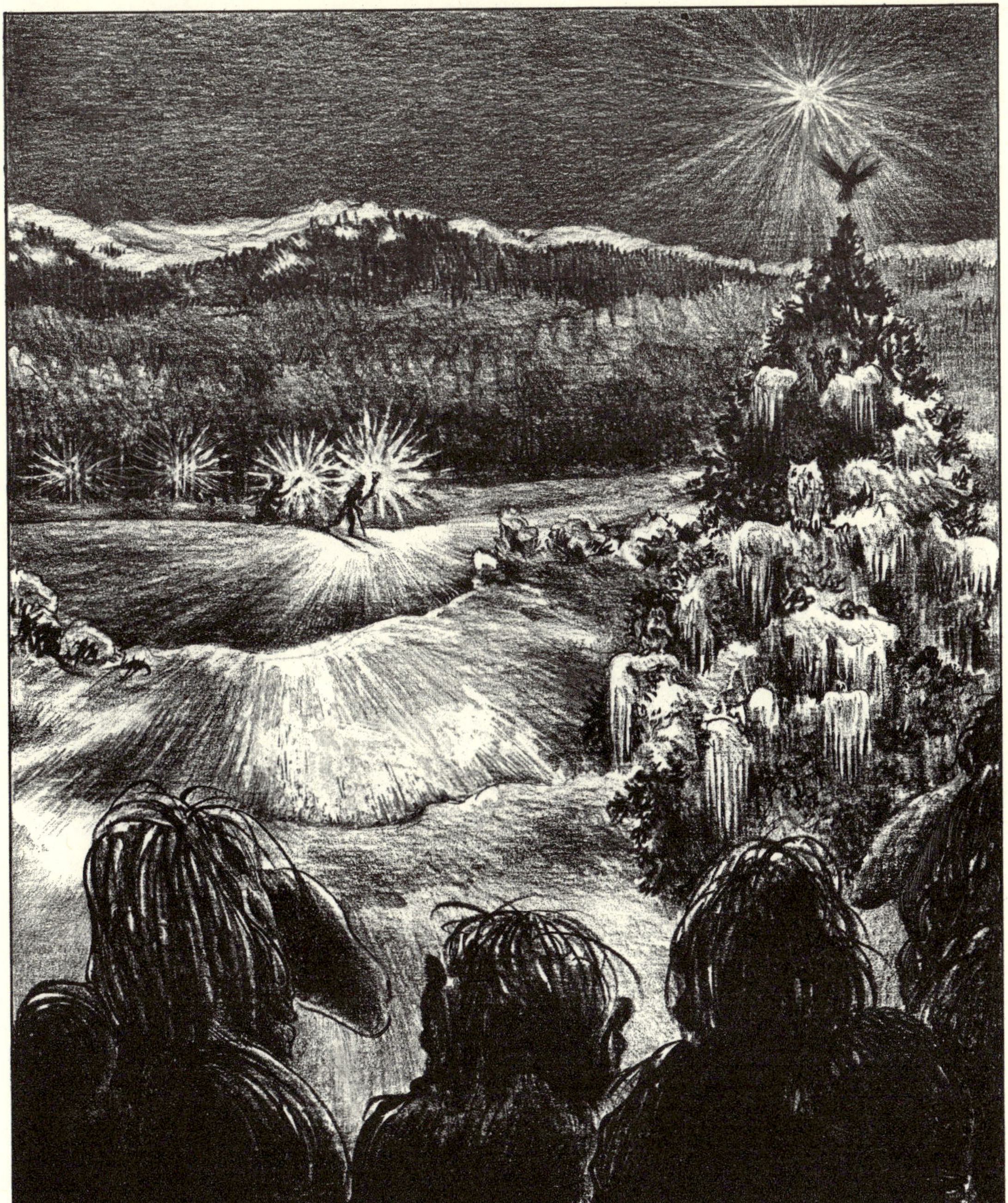

themselves were trying to dance like the humans, while the humans were trying to dance like the animals.

On and on they danced through the night, on and on until the stars grew dim. Finally Langemann tripped over Nesa's nose. You see, it had grown longer with happiness since the evening began and now they all fell over it, laughing in the snow.

And so the dancing came to an end. Panting and smiling, everyone moved back around the tree. They waited in the dark for their breathing to calm. The forest grew still, and a soft sort of peace settled over them all. Now their breathing gently frosted and faded, frosted and faded, without a sound.

A pale rim of light began to outline Jughandle.

"Ee-da-how," whispered several voices.

And just as they said it, a strange thing happened! They turned to one another, trolls, animals, and humans, and began to speak in a new language that all could understand! The words were like the snow which comes soundlessly covering all, soft words which it takes no words to say, but which speak as clearly as dawn breaking over the mountain.

And as they stood there in Ee-da-how's glow, these are the words they heard Dovergubben say: "God morgan! God jul and Merry Christmas! At last our trolldom is complete. No matter the day, or weather, or season, this forest—Trollhaven—will be our home!"

He paused and gazed around the circle. "Sure as we stand together now, so surely must some venture forth in time. But no matter! No matter the time or distance! It's to one trolldom we all belong!"

And So . . .

And so when spring melted Trollhaven's last snows, the white-haired man set forth on his expedition. True to his word, he took Rolfus with him, promising to return ere the troll baby was grown.

In the woods and meadows around Little Lake, trolls, animals, and humans are learning each other's ways. Wherever the river runs, it whispers their story, and wherever the wind blows, it carries their songs. Some say that Trollhaven is even talked of in the town, for more and more people are beginning to believe in trolls. So too the trolls are coming to believe in people, in a way they never did before.

At night around the fire, the trolls and their friends lift their heads and listen to the wind. Perhaps it will blow in a song from the north, bearing news of Rolfus and the white-haired man. Where are they now? Are they with the bald eagles at Great Slave Lake? Or have they gone on, across the Arctic to the place where the three rivers meet? Have they climbed Troll Tinderne to meet with Storegubben and the rest? Has the tale of the search for Trollhaven been told?

If so, it could be that more trolls have set forth from Norway, following their noses to—who knows where? After all, the Master Troll had said that if Dovergubben and his Viking trolls were successful, others might go traveling too! And perhaps even now, in the forests and the meadows, by the lakes and along the streams of many lands, trolls are finding places where they can feel at home.

So the next time you go for a walk in the woods, or climb a mountain or camp by a lake, look between the light and the shadows. Look through the curtains the river makes, as it sparkles and tumbles over the rocks. If you sit quietly, if you breathe gently, who can say what you may see? Who can say what you may hear? Listen . . .

*To the people of McCall,
especially Bunny,
and to Anne and Benjamin,
who make the trolls happy.*

Guide to Norwegian Pronunciation

(Stress the syllable that is in *italics*.)

björn	(b'yurn)
Dovergubben	(*duh*vur-goob'n)
Eggöya	(*egg*ew-yah)
en, to, tre, fire, fem, seks	(en, tew, tray, *fee*ruh, fem, seks)
farvel	(*far*rvel)
fest	(fest)
fjord	(f'yord)
fjell	(f'yell)
Fosina	(fah*see*nah)
Fosekallen	(*fah*suhkahl'n)
Fridtjof Nansen	(*freet*yahf *nahns*'n)
Gaustad	(*gahw*stahd)
god dag	(good dahg)
god Jul	(good yewl)
god morgen	(good *morg*'n)
Gudbrandsdalen	(*gewd*-brahnz-dahl'n)
Hardanger	(*harr*-dahng'r)
havhest	(*hahv*-hest)

himmel	(*himm*'l)
hvallross	(*vahl*-rahss)
hypp	(hip)
ja	(yah)
Jan Mayen	(yahn mine)
Jotulen	(*yo*-tewl'n)
juletre	(*yewl*tray)
Kari	(*kar*ree)
Kjerringa	(*shahr*-ringah)
Kalvehalen	(*kahl*vuh-hahl'n)
Ladoga	(*lah*dogah)
Langemann	(*lahng*-uhmahn)
Leif Ericson	(lyf *a*iriks'n)
Lesja	(*lesh*a)
Lom	(lom)
Lund	(loond)
Lungyer	(*loong*yur)
mange takk	(*mahng*-uhtahk)
min elskede	(meen *ell*skeduh)
Mjösa	(*m'yo*suh)
Nesa	(*nay*suh)
Nökken	(*nuhk*'n)
Nökkina	(nuh*keen*uh)

171

Nökkungen	(*nuhk*-kung'n)
Norge	(*norr*guh)
og	(ahg)
Oslo	(*ahs*slo)
Revesmuget	(*revv*uhss-*mew*guh)
Roald Amundsen	(*ro*-ahl *ah*muns'n)
Rumpungen	(*rewm*-pung'n)
slott	(slaht)
Sperillen	(*spair*ilun)
Storegubben	(*storr*-uhgoob'n)
Svalbard	(*svahl*bar)
Tåkeheimen	(*tok*uh-haym'n)
Tinderne	(*tin*durnuh)
tusen takk	(*tew*sun tahk)
Vågå	(vogo)
Valdermon	(*vahll*durmahn)
Valdres	(*vahll*druhss)
Vally	(*vah*lee)
Vänern	(*vuhn*urn)
vaskebjörn	(*vahss*kuh-b'yurn)
velkommen	(*vell*-komen)
velkomstfest	(*vell*-komst-fest)
vidunderlig	(vee-*dun*-derlee)

The Authors

Odd Bjerke grew up in Norway and graduated from the University of Oslo with a degree in Arctic Ecology. He has spent most of his life exploring the North, mapping unknown areas and studying the birds, animals, and plants that live in them. He also teaches others the skills they need to live safely in the wilderness. When he is not on an expedition, Mr. Bjerke lives near Trollhaven.

After studying playwriting at the University of Michigan, **Meredith Motson** began working with children's theater in the small mountain town of McCall, Idaho. It was there that she met Odd Bjerke and began writing down the tale he told her of the trolls who left Norway to find a home in the New World.